NOTRE DAME GAME DAY

NOTRE DAME GAME DAY

Getting There, Getting in, and
Getting in the Spirit

TODD TUCKER

Foreword by Lou Holtz

Diamond Communications, Inc.
South Bend, Indiana

NOTRE DAME GAME DAY:
Getting There, Getting in, and Getting in the Spirit
Copyright © 2000 by Todd Tucker

10 9 8 7 6 5 4 3 2 1

Manufactured in the United States of America

Diamond Communications, Inc.
Post Office Box 88
South Bend, Indiana 46624-0088
Editorial: (219) 299-9278
Fax: (219) 299-9296
Orders Only: 1-800-480-3717
Website: www.diamondbooks.com

Library of Congress Cataloging-in-Publication Data

Tucker, Todd, 1968-
    Notre Dame game day : getting there, getting in, and getting in
    the spirit / by Todd Tucker
        p. cm.
    ISBN 1-888698-30-6
    1. Notre Dame Fighting Irish (Football team) 2. Football fans.
    3. University of Notre Dame—Football—History. I. Title.

GV958.U54 T83 2000
796.332'63'0977289--dc21
                                                        00-063893

TABLE OF CONTENTS

Acknowledgments ix

Publisher's Note x

Foreword xi

Chapter One • Why You Should Go 1

•Numbers You Should Know: .881
  College Football's Winningest Coach 3

Chapter Two • The Irish Sweepstakes: Getting Tickets 5

•Numbers You Should Know: 4
  The Four Horsemen 14

Chapter Three • Drive North, Stop at Dome: Getting There 16

•Numbers You Should Know: 1928
  The Gipper 29

Chapter Four • From the Concierge Floor to the Dorm
  Room Floor: Lodging 31

•Numbers You Should Know: 0-0
  The 1946 Army Game 63

Chapter Five • New Museum Proves Other Teams Exist:
  The College Football Hall of Fame 65

•Numbers You Should Know: 10-10
  The 1966 Michigan State Game 77

Chapter Six • Keeping the Game Day Body and Soul Together:
  Food and Drink 79

•Numbers You Should Know: 11
Notre Dame's National Championships 101

Chapter Seven • Number One Moses and Touchdown Jesus:
A Walking Tour 103

•Numbers You Should Know: 7
Notre Dame's Seven Heisman Trophy Winners 124

Chapter Eight • Warm Beer at Sunrise: Pre-game 127

•Numbers You Should Know: 27 seconds
Daniel "Rudy" Ruettiger 141

Chapter Nine • Four Quarters of Tradition: In the Stadium 142

•Numbers You Should Know: 2
New Traditions 155

Chapter Ten • After the Game 158

Campus Map 162

Stadium Seating 167

Future Schedules 169

About the Author 170

Index 171

For my little girls

Colleen, Class of 2015, and Shannon, Class of 2020

ACKNOWLEDGMENTS

AS IS THE CASE with every decent thing I have accomplished as an adult, I could not have written this book without Susie, my wife, at my side. Thank you for everything.

I would also like to thank several members of the Notre Dame family. John Heisler, the Sports Information Director, was unfailingly helpful to me from the very beginning, despite my suspicious lack of credentials. Heisler is a national champion in his own right—his media guide has been judged the best in the country eight times. He is also a good guy in the greatest Irish tradition. Thanks to Dennis K. Moore and Richard Conklin, who both have been helping me since this book was only an outline. I also owe a special thanks to the great Dave Prentkowski, the Director of Notre Dame Food Services. In addition to completely restructuring his organization to better serve students, Dave gave me two hours of his valuable time, and a cup of coffee, on a holiday weekend. Finally, thank you to Coach Lou Holtz, both for writing the foreword, and for winning the National Championship during my junior year. You are having an incredible year, Coach, and you deserve it.

Many people outside the university also helped me with this book. John Parsons, the Marketing Director for the Northern Indiana Commuter Transportation District, went out of his way to help me learn about the living history that is the South Shore Railroad. Carolyne Wallace of the Varsity Clubs of America earned my undying gratitude with her hospitality, and by introducing me to Eddie Robinson. A special thanks also to Jill Langford of Diamond Communications. Jill, more than anyone I know, represents what a Notre Dame graduate is supposed to be.

Finally, a special thanks Mishawaka's Beth Reising—my mother-in-law. She is Notre Dame's biggest fan, and I am hers. In the last year, she has acted has my unpaid assistant in this project, culling the local newspapers for useful articles, suggesting topics, and watching the kids while Susie and I went to games. I don't know if she'll ever know how helpful all this has been.

A PUBLISHER'S NOTE (or two)

I WOULD LIKE TO take some space to recognize a few people. First of all, author Todd Tucker, whose enthusiasm, good spirits, sense of humor, and *patience* made the editorial/production process a pleasure. Next up for kudos, Diamond Communications' graphic designer, Juanita Dix who went beyond her artistic duty to get this book to press. Jonathan Reeder, Notre Dame sophomore for the impromptu but enjoyable tour of the new Warren Golf Course. I'm sorry the photo of you on #4 green didn't make the cut. ND senior photographer, Peter Richardson—thank you for answering my calls and e-mails and coming through with some last-minute shots for the book. And my right-hand, Shari Hill, assistant to a sometimes crazed publisher, for her fact checking, input, and other helpful duties too numerous to list here.

Special thanks to Coach Lou Holtz for writing the foreword to *Notre Dame Game Day*. When it came to putting THE GAME in the day each fall Saturday at Notre Dame, Coach knew how to do it. Continued success at the University of South Carolina, Coach, as you give more fans reason to bring down the goalposts!

And, finally, I'd like to especially thank Dick Conklin, public relations director of the University of Notre Dame, for his cooperation with this effort. His faith that a Domer author with a Domer publisher would produce a sensible publication is much appreciated.

I would like to point out, though, that this book makes no claim to being an official publication of the University of Notre Dame and, therefore, does not necessarily represent the views and opinions of the university. The book is intended to be a guide to making the most of a Notre Dame home football game weekend. However, both author and publisher hope that, while enjoyment is the desired goal, the game-goer's fun will always be guided by common sense and concern for personal safety as well as the safety of others.

Have fun! Be safe! Go Irish!
JILL A. LANGFORD

FOREWORD

I COULD HAVE USED a book like this on September 13, 1986—the day that I coached my first game as Notre Dame's head coach. As a matter of fact, I could have used a book like this all that week. Even though I had been a fan of the Irish ever since the nuns of St. Aloysius Grade School marched me out to recess to the tune of the "Notre Dame Victory March," I had only been to two Notre Dame games before that day—I am normally pretty busy on Saturday afternoons. So, many of the rituals and ceremonies that filled that day, that week, and that season were as new to me as they were to the wide-eyed freshmen that had arrived on campus about the same that I did. You can take it from me when I tell you that it is hard for the uninitiated to understand the quality and the quantity of activities that surround a home football game at the University of Notre Dame. Todd has done an admirable job here in trying to convey the details of that experience.

Two-hundred-fifty people attended a luncheon we gave before my first game. That number grew to 3,000 by my third year and stayed there throughout my time at Notre Dame. Thousands of people watched our practices. More attended the pep rally in Stepan Center on Friday night. Giant recreational vehicles lumbered onto Green Field three days before the game. By Friday, they were part of an armada of tailgaters that formed a defensive perimeter around the campus. Even painting the helmets on Friday night was a ritual, as the older student managers supervised the work of the gold-stained managers-in-training. By the time a formation of Air Force A-10 bombers buzzed the stadium during the crescendo of the National Anthem, I had reached the conclusion that this was a pretty big deal.

About those campers that showed up days early for the game: I saw something in those fans that I have never seen anywhere else. I learned that many of these fans wandered the campus, prayed at the Grotto, and spent money at the bookstore, just as you would expect from any fans. When kickoff arrived, though, they went inside their campers to watch the game on television—they didn't have tickets. They weren't frustrated by this, or disappointed—entering the stadium had never been a part of their plans. They were just happy to be on the campus of the University of Notre Dame during a football weekend. Those fans realized something that this book makes clear—there are a lot of things to do during a game weekend outside the stadium walls.

Because of the great demand for tickets, few people outside the student body get to attend every game. In a way, this makes the students the caretakers of the traditions inside the stadium, from game to game and from season to season. At no other school will you see such a close bond between the athletes on the field and the students in the stands. When people come to their first Notre Dame game, this is often the thing they remember the most—the sight of the student section standing for four quarters of football.

Todd Tucker does a fine job within these pages describing the wealth of activities that surround a Notre Dame game. This is obviously a great help to fans on their way to a game. It is also a good read for those of us who have fond memories of games inside that stadium from seasons past. Notre Dame games are nice things to remember. On a fall weekend, when the leaves are turning, the band is playing, and the stands are filled with singing fans, Notre Dame is the most beautiful place on earth.

LOU HOLTZ

Chapter One

WHY YOU SHOULD GO

NOTRE DAME FANS are orphans. We are in every state and a multitude of countries, but we are concentrated nowhere. Even just a few miles from campus, you are just as likely to see a Purdue banner or a Michigan bumper sticker, as you are to see some sign of loyalty to the Irish. Notre Dame fans walk alone through life, or at best in small, dedicated bands, as regional loyalties predominate, no matter what region you happen to be in.

With students from all 50 states, Notre Dame is America's most national university. Although the campus is in Indiana, Indiana is not the largest contributor to the student body—California is, followed by New York. Indiana places third. You hear an interesting mix of accents on campus, from the warm drawl of New Orleans, to the staccato of Long Island, to the distinctive speech patterns of Chicago, from which all the great Midwestern accents are derived. The student body returns to the nation at large upon graduation, which results in a national presence, but few strongholds. In Alabama, most three-year-olds can tell you Bear Bryant's win-loss record. While many of us can name Notre Dame's seven Heisman Trophy winners, we usually don't have that many people to share that information with.

Our friends know that we are Notre Dame fans, and regard us as oddities. When someone new comes to the office that likes Notre Dame, he'll hear, "You like Notre Dame? You should meet Bob, he likes Notre Dame, too." A similar conversation would not take place in Huntsville, where loyalty to the Crimson Tide would be presumed, and would probably be a condition of employment. Being a Notre Dame fan can be lonely. Except, of course, on game day.

Eighty thousand of us gather then. A nation of us watches every home game on NBC, courtesy of college football's only such contract. You become aware that you are not alone. In the parking lots, every car flies a giant ND flag. At home, your favorite Notre Dame sweatshirt is a novelty, and elicits comments from strangers in the mall. In the stadium, you are in a sea of Notre Dame apparel, from the famous plaid pants of the old men to the tiny cheerleader outfits worn by the babies in their strollers. At Notre Dame on game day, you realize that you are not alone. You are part of an army.

In 1997, the army grew in size by about 20,000 people for every game—the result of the stadium expansion. While every game still is an immediate sell-out, this overall larger pool of tickets has made it easier than ever to attend a game. Even so, the number of hotel rooms in the area remains shockingly small, and the number of bar stools and flights into South Bend has remained relatively constant. As a direct result of the stadium expansion, the number of parking spaces has actually decreased. So, getting a ticket to a Notre Dame game is easier than ever. Everything else is harder. I will attempt, in this book, to help.

As with any army, Notre Dame fans possess a set of rituals, a language, and a mythology all their own. This book, I hope, will do more than just give you the phone numbers for area hotels and a stadium seating chart. I hope to introduce you to the layers of tradition that make up a Notre Dame football weekend. Even if you don't ever get to go to a game, learning these traditions will give you a better understanding of one of America's great institutions. After learning about all of the pomp, the ritual, and the fun of a fall weekend at Notre Dame, though, you will want to go. And you should. It's important.

Numbers you should know: .881

College Football's Winningest Coach

Knute Rockne is more than the patron saint of Irish football. His motivational skill, his innovation, and his considerable flair for promotion turned college football into a national sport.

Born on March 4, 1888, in Voss, Norway, Rockne's family immigrated to Chicago in 1893. He enrolled at Notre Dame in 1910. While there, he wrote for the school newspaper, played flute in the orchestra, was a campus marbles champion, and set a school record in the pole vault. Rockne also managed to graduate Magna cum Laude with a degree in chemistry. After graduation, Rockne stayed on to be an assistant in the chemistry department, and an assistant to the football coach, Jesse Harper. When Harper retired in 1917, the 29-year-old Rockne took over as head coach. In his 13-year career as Notre Dame's head coach, Rockne changed the game of college football forever.

• His career record was 105-12-5, for a career winning percentage of .881—the best in the history of the sport. Second place, incidentally, belongs to Frank Leahy, who played for Rockne.

• He developed the dreaded "Notre Dame Shift," an offense so effective that it was eventually banned.

• He was the first head coach to make the forward pass a standard part of his offense.

• Rockne began Notre Dame's great rivalry with the University of Southern California. By creating college football's first national rivalry, Rockne turned the sport into a national institution.

After the first season in the stadium that he designed, Knute Rockne was travelling to Los Angeles to participate in a promotional film about college football. On March 31, 1931, the plane he was on, Transcontinental-Western Flight 599, crashed near Bazaar, Kansas, killing all onboard.

Photo courtesy of the University of Notre Dame Photography

Chapter Two

THE IRISH SWEEPSTAKES:
Getting Tickets

GETTING TICKETS TO A Notre Dame football game is easy. First, apply for admission to the university.

Notre Dame, unlike almost every other big-time program, still guarantees every student a ticket to every home game. The rest of us have to fight with each other over a very limited supply. After students, alumni have the best shot at tickets, followed by the parents of students, who are guaranteed tickets to at least one game a year. Members of the general public will have the hardest time acquiring tickets, although, as this chapter will show, it is far from impossible. The face value of every ticket is $36. Unless you are buying your tickets directly from the university, though, the cold laws of supply-and-demand will dictate your actual price. That demand is huge: Notre Dame has sold out every home game since a Thanksgiving Day match-up with Air Force in 1973.

The university allocates tickets with the rigor of a lifeboat captain rationing food. The official distribution is as follows:

Group	Allotment
Students	11,000
Faculty/Staff	7,000
Opponents	5,000

Season Tickets	16,000
University Allotments	9,000
Contributing Alumni	32,000

Season tickets are interesting—the university doesn't sell new ones anymore. They did once, though, and they sold those tickets with the understanding that holders would be able to renew them indefinitely, a promise the university continues to honor. Season tickets can be transferred once every 10 years for a fee. If the original season ticket holder dies, or fails to pay the renewal fee, then the season ticket goes away, and the seats are returned to the general admission pool. So, even though 16,000 seats are reserved by season ticket holders, season tickets are really no longer for sale.

"University Allotments" refers to trustees, advisory council members, and major benefactors. If you are not sure whether or not you belong to this group, you don't. Here are the details on getting tickets for the rest of us: alumni, parents, and the general public.

ALUMNI

The lottery is the university's official ticket distribution system for alumni. To be eligible for the lottery, alumni must be "active contributors" to the university—the minimum amount varies with the year of graduation. Alumni who graduated since 1993 must contribute at least $50 annually. Members of the classes of 1950-1993 must contribute at least $100. If you graduated before 1950, the requirement drops back down to $50.

There is a widespread misconception that alumni receive in the mail every year a solicitation that says, in effect, "send this card in with $100 to participate in the ticket lottery." The university, you can be sure, does track each donation, but they do not solicit it. Alumni are supposed to know the rules, and make their required donation without crass reminders. Of course, the onset of football season without any tickets is a great reminder. Although any contribution to a recognized campus group counts toward the requirement, most alumni give during the Annual Fund Drive. This donation can be mailed to:

University of Notre Dame
Annual Fund
110 Grace Hall
Notre Dame, IN 46556

This donation is not applied towards the cost of your tickets—it just makes you eligible for the lottery. Alumni who have not participated for many years are always eligible to jump back into the system—just send your donation to the above address.

Alumni who make the proper donation will receive their lottery applications in February or early March. You may apply for as many tickets as you like, but you must include a check for the entire amount. You will receive a refund good for the amount of the tickets that you do not receive. The lottery application is due every year on May 16. You can call the Alumni Office at 219-631-7959 for more information about getting in or staying in the lottery.

Networking for tickets is one of the great advantages of staying active in your regional alumni club. If you don't have tickets for the game you want, someone else in the club probably will. It is customary, in alumni-to-alumni deals, to charge only face value.

Students at St. Mary's College receive the exact same student tickets that Notre Dame students do. They pay the same prices, and wait in the same line. Upon graduation, though, St. Mary's alumni are not eligible for the lottery. The discrepancy receives surprisingly little attention.

PARENTS

Once a year, the university reserves a block of tickets for parents of students for a couple of games, to show its gratitude for the thousands of dollars that they have paid in tuition. This is traditionally for the easiest couple of games of the year. It is a rare opportunity, though, for non-alumni to get guaranteed tickets at face value. Parents should seriously consider taking advantage of this privilege, as it will disappear promptly upon their child's graduation.

GENERAL PUBLIC

There are three basic sources of tickets for the general public: the university, ticket brokers, and scalpers.

Ticket scalping, despite what you will hear, is legal in Indiana. It is, however, against the rules on the campus of the University of Notre Dame. Ticket holders who cannot use their tickets are supposed to return them to the ticket window at the east side of the stadium—the side that faces the JACC—where they will be resold at face value. Often there are a surprising number of tickets available at the east window on game day. The window opens three hours before kickoff. For big games, the line forms much earlier. For many games, tickets remain at kickoff. Before paying a premium to a scalper, visit the east window.

Photo credit: Susie & Todd Tucker

Since the stadium expansion, Notre Dame also has a few tickets available in advance, through the ticket office. This is because for so many years calling the ticket office has been futile—most fans either have given up, or are not even aware of this option. In the 1998 home opener against Michigan, tickets were available from the ticket office until the Thursday before the game. You can call the ticket office at 219-631-7356 to check on availability.

Ticket brokers have a strange, symbiotic relationship with the university. For many fans, brokers are an important source of tickets. For many important season-ticket-holding alumni, ticket brokers are an easy way to unload unneeded tickets. The university, though, doesn't like anyone outside to make money with the tickets, so it tries to make it sound illegal. Ticket brokering, in fact, is legal in Indiana, as in most states. It is even somewhat regulated, protecting the interests of both buyers and sellers.

Brokers, on the other hand, often claim an official tie to the university—none exists. Brokers get their tickets from season ticket holders, not the university, and sell them at a highly inflated price. Brokers are plentiful on the Internet. They also buy ads in the sports sections of almost every American newspaper—Notre Dame tickets are most heavily marketed in the *Chicago Tribune*, and the *South Bend Tribune*. Here are the responses from three major brokers, and their prices for one high demand game, LSU, and one low demand game, Baylor.

Who Needs Two?
• HYPERLINK http://www.ticketbroker.com
888-246-8499
Baylor tickets: $100
LSU Tickets: $300
Premiere Tickets and Tours
• HYPERLINK http://www.gottickets.com
800-775-1617
Baylor tickets: $135 (in the end zone)
LSU tickets: $400 (between the 35 yardlines)
Front Row Tickets and Tours
• HYPERLINK http://www.exepc.com
800-878-1939
Baylor tickets: $125
LSU tickets: $300

Besides giving a snapshot picture of market prices for some tickets, this informal survey proves one other important point: all the brokers had tickets available for every game. This is the bottom line with brokers. They can get you the tickets you want—for a price.

Closely related to the ticket brokers are the travel agents who book vacation packages to Notre Dame games. These kinds of packages originated with bowl games, expanded into away games, and now include home games. Customers purchase a complete package, which usually includes two nights in a hotel, maybe a rental car, and, of course, tickets. Travel agents who specialize in these packages advertise heavily in the Notre Dame fan publications, like the *Irish Sports Report*, and *Blue and Gold Illustrated*. Some of the bigger agencies are:

Anthony Travel
1-800-7DOMERS
Typical package includes: tickets, two nights lodging, transportation to the game, and a tailgater hosted by the agency.
Price: $339 per person
Redden Travel
1-800-466-0153
Typical package includes: tickets and two nights lodging.
Price: $499 per person
PJ's Sports Tours
1-888-416-9408
Typical package includes: tickets, two nights lodging, breakfast on game day, and a campus tour.
Price: $349 per person.

There are two kinds of scalpers—regular folks who have an extra ticket or two, and professionals. Professional scalpers are a step below brokers on the food chain—the scalper's office is in the median of Highway 31. While brokers operate under at least a modicum of regulation, scalpers are a wholly unfettered manifestation of free enterprise. Some tips for working with professional scalpers:

Read the tickets carefully—verify that you're not getting great seats for last week's game. If you are paying for two seats together, read the numbers on the tickets, and verify that they are indeed together.

Haggle—a business professor at Notre Dame once told me to never accept the first offer. It remains great advice, no matter what the pursuit.

Wait until kickoff—as the band warms up, the prices will drop like a stone.

Any area of high fan traffic will attract scalpers, but the traditional gathering place is on Highway 31, at the Toll Road's Notre Dame exit. The scalper will be easy to recognize—he's the one with a giant wad of tickets in one hand, and a giant wad of cash in the other. Scalpers can also be found at the College Football Hall of Fame, and in most hotel lobbies on Saturday morning.

Regular folks with extra tickets to sell can be harder to spot, but are generally nicer to deal with. Keep your eyes open in the tailgating areas and around the stadium, but be discreet when making the drop. Remember that while scalping is legal in the state's eyes, it is against Notre Dame policy. *Each Notre Dame ticket states on the back that it may not be "offered for resale on Notre Dame premises." Note that this is against the rules even if the ticket is offered at face value.* The policy further states that if such reselling is detected, the tickets will be confiscated and the sellers will be escorted off campus. Ticket privileges can be revoked from the original ticket holder of record. Like many university policies, this one is unevenly enforced. Sometimes, scalpers hawk their wares at the stadium gates like carnival barkers. Other times, the university will warn people who simply hold tickets above their heads. Be careful.

A quick word about student tickets: Notre Dame, St. Mary's, and Holy Cross students are the only authorized users of student tickets. A student ID is supposed to be presented with the ticket. Shortly before kickoff, though, when the crush is on, students pore through the gates without presenting their IDs. It is a risky, undertaking though, for people who are obviously not of student age to attempt entry with student tickets. Beware the student scalper.

Unless that student has regular General Admission tickets for sale, which does happen. Sometimes students have their parents' unused Parents' Day tickets, or their parents are season ticket holders. When buying tickets from students, you have the added advantage of their generally desperate need for cash. The best place to find these tickets is in the classified ad section of Notre Dame's student newspaper,

The Observer. The paper is published five days a week, and you can subscribe to it for $85 a year. In addition to being a valuable ticket-finding resource, the paper has an historically fine sports section, and is one of the best ways to track ND athletics. To subscribe, contact: The Observer, P.O. Box Q, Notre Dame IN 46556, 219-631-7471.

No matter how you get tickets, whether through the lottery or from a scalper on the highway median, your work will be easier if you choose a game that is in low demand. The experience will be no less enjoyable. The events and activities that make up a Notre Dame football weekend take place for every home game, not just those against a mighty rival like Michigan. Notre Dame's schedule is always among the nation's toughest, but the few patsies on it can make your search for tickets considerably easier. In addition, you will be (almost) guaranteed an Irish victory. Here are the weakest matchups for the next three seasons:

November 17, 2001	Navy
November 23, 2002	Rutgers
October 4, 2003	Wake Forest
November 8, 2003	Navy

It's a tie

Alumni have benefited the most from the expanded stadium: 76% of the new seats have been earmarked for them. The increased supply, though, has eased the pressure on everyone. Brokers always have tickets, and the ticket office sometimes does, for those fans who need to get their tickets well in advance. Don't be afraid to go to South Bend without tickets, though. For all but the biggest matchups, you will be able to find tickets, either from the university, other fans, or from scalpers.

A GAME THAT NEVER SELLS OUT:
THE BLUE AND GOLD GAME

Notre Dame's annual spring scrimmage is the Blue and Gold Game. It is held every spring as a fundraiser for the Notre Dame Club of St. Joseph County, and it never sells out.

The Blue and Gold Game is to ND football what Spring Training is to Major League Baseball. The crowd is laid back, the weather is nice, and the stakes are low. It does give fans a chance to see next year's team in full pads, in the stadium. The game has drawn at least 20,000 fans to the stadium for the last eight straight contests.

Call the ticket office at 219-631-7356 for more information. Tickets are $8 on game day, $6 in advance. Future dates for the Blue and Gold game are: April 28, 2001 and April 27, 2002.

HANDICAPPED TICKETS AND PARKING

One of the great benefits of the stadium expansion is that the refurbished stadium is now truly compliant with the Americans with Disabilities Act.

Handicapped seats go on sale on June 30. The ticket allows the holder and one escort to sit in the wheelchair area. These areas are now located all around the stadium, and on both levels. The elevator is located by gates 10 and 110—right by the ticket office. Alumni who are requesting wheelchair seating must request it on their ticket applications.

Handicapped parking is available on a drive-up basis around the stadium, with a proper handicapped parking tag or permit. You can also guarantee yourself a handicapped space for $20. Call the ticket office at 219-631-7356 for more information.

Numbers you should know: 4

The Four Horsemen

"Outlined against a blue, gray October sky the Four Horsemen rode again. In dramatic lore they are known as famine, pestilence, destruction, and death. These are only aliases. Their real names are Stuhldreher, Miller, Crowley, and Layden."—Grantland Rice, *New York Herald Tribune*, October 19, 1924

Soon after the *New York Herald Tribune* published these words, George Strickler, Knute Rockne's quick-thinking publicity aide, borrowed four horses from a South Bend livery stable and took a photograph of the four players on horseback, each with a football and a leather helmet. Their lasting fame is a tribute to both Rockne's formidable promotional skills, and to the power of Grantland Rice's words.

To be fair to the players, though, the Four Horsemen were more than a media creation. The four of them played 30 games as a unit, and lost to only one team—Nebraska. The famed backfield was undefeated during the season that Rice named them. They went on to beat Stanford in the 1925 Rose Bowl in their last game together, winning the National Championship.

The Four Horsemen were:

    Harry Stuhldreher – Quarterback

    Jim Crowley – Left Halfback

    Don Miller – Right Halfback

    Elmer Layden – Fullback

The Four Horsemen: Don Miller, Elmer Layden, Jim Crowley, Harry Stuhldreher. Photo courtesy of the University of Notre Dame Photography Department

Chapter Three

DRIVE NORTH, STOP AT DOME:
Getting There

WHEN FATHER SORIN journeyed to the wilds of northern Indiana to found Notre Dame in 1842, he wanted solitude. Inaccessibility is desirable to prayerful scholars—the Amish settled in the region for much the same reason. Notre Dame football fans come to South Bend for a different sort of religious experience, however. While today's fan has many transportation options, Notre Dame's remote location and snowy climate can still cause a travelling fan headaches. Father Sorin would be happy to see that the trip north is still challenging—it's a pilgrimage, after all.

PLANES

The Michiana Regional Airport has undergone some major fan-friendly changes in the last decade. It is now a regional transportation hub, with train and bus terminals built right into the facility. The South Shore Train terminal moved from its dismal location on the city's West Side to the airport in 1992—more about that later. In 1994, the small airport completed a $4.5 million expansion that greatly enhanced not only the airport's service, but its overall pleasantness as well. The airport is now served by eight airlines.

On game day, Transpo, the South Bend city bus service, runs continuous express service between the airport and the stadium—it costs

Photo credit: Sue & Todd Tucker

$5 each way. All busses pick passengers up at the far western end of the airport—the same end as the "Cafe SBN" restaurant.

Flyers have another option. United Limousine, a Mishawaka-based bus company, runs busses almost continuously between Chicago's major airports and the Notre Dame campus. The busses are clean and generally filled with convivial fans. A trip on the bus is $28 one way, or $52 for the round trip. You can call 1-800-254-5000 for information, but no reservations are required for the trips between Chicago and the campus. United Limo has been making this trip every hour since 1979, and they have gotten pretty good at it. Just like the Transpo city busses, United Limo busses can be found at the far western end of the airport.

Taking the bus from Midway or O'Hare makes sense for several reasons. On a game weekend, it can be expensive to fly to South Bend, if plane tickets are available at all. Direct flights to Chicago are available from almost anywhere in the country. Often, these direct flights will be significantly cheaper than a complete trip to South Bend. Lastly, some people are made nervous by the tiny planes that fly into South Bend. The tiny planes, sometimes called "puddle jumpers," are loud and offer some occasionally hair-raising turbulence. Some fans, when making the 45-minute flight in one of these flying Winnebagos, can't help but recall Rockne's untimely death. For these fans, the 90-minute bus ride may be a soothing option.

AIRLINES SERVING MICHIANA REGIONAL

American Eagle	800-433-7300
ATA Connection	800-225-2995
Continental Express	800-525-0280
Delta Connection	800-221-1212
(Comair, Delta & ASA)	
Northwest/KLM	800-225-2525
TWA Express/TWA	800-221-2000
United Express	800-241-6522
US Airways/US Air Express	800-428-4322/800-428-4322

CITIES WITH DIRECT FLIGHTS TO SOUTH BEND

CITY	AIRLINE
Atlanta	Delta Connection (ASA)
Chicago O'Hare	United, American Eagle
Chicago Midway	ATA
Cincinnati	Delta Connection (Comair)
Cleveland	Continental Express
Detroit	Northwest/KLM
Pittsburgh	US Airways
St. Louis	TW Express

TRAINS

The Chicago Cubs have the el, the New York Yankees have the subway, and Notre Dame has the South Shore. If there is an "authentic" way to get to a Notre Dame game, it is aboard this historic train.

A brief history: The South Shore began in 1903 as part of a wave of interurban electric trains that served the eastern half of the United States. Like almost everything else, the train line went bankrupt during the depression. The South Shore was reorganized and reopened just in time to experience its most profitable period ever during World War II. Over six million people a year rode the train to the steel mills that lined Lake Michigan during the war. When the war ended, though, GI's were buying cars and moving to the suburbs, and ridership began a long, steady

18

Photo credit: Susie & Todd Tucker

decline. By 1977, the line's private owners wanted to give up on passenger service altogether.

The government stepped in, but not in time to prevent another bankruptcy. The state purchased all of the South Shore's assets at auction, and, by 1990, the train system was completely in the hands of the public sector. With a glorious disregard for profits, the government has poured money into the South Shore, buying modern railcars and improving the stations. While the South Shore has certainly had its fiscal ups and downs, it holds the distinction of being the only electric interurban train in the United States still operating. Almost four million passengers rode the South Shore in 1998.

For Notre Dame fans, the greatest improvement to the system occurred in 1992, when the terminal was moved from South Bend's less-than-scenic West Side to its present location at the airport. I once had a friend who spent a weekend in Chicago, leaving his car at the old train station. When he returned, his car was on fire. It was that kind of place. Be warned: Amtrak passengers still pass through the scary old station. South Shore passengers no longer need to feel mortal fear—at least not in South Bend.

Randolph Street in downtown Chicago is one end of the South Shore line; South Bend is the other. Travelling the entire length of the

Photo credit: Susie & Todd Tucker

South Shore line takes two hours and 20 minutes, and costs $9.40, one way. On weekends, up to two children 13 years old or younger, when accompanied by parents, can ride free. The train can make up to 18 stops in between Chicago and South Bend.

Seven trains a day make the trip Monday through Friday, while nine trains a day make the trip on weekends and holidays—this reflects the train's change of status from mainly a commuter vehicle to a recreational one.

At the center each train car is a restroom made of shiny stainless steel like an airplane's, although the train's restroom is bigger. Seats on one side of the restroom face forward, while seats on the other end face backwards. Also near the restroom are a water fountain and a credit card-operated telephone. Passengers must pay their fare onboard the train, and only cash is accepted. The carry-on restrictions are similar to an airplane's—your bags must fit into an overhead compartment. After arriving at the South Bend airport, fans can catch an express city bus right to the stadium for $5.00. South Shore officials assure me that game day trains are never, never sold out.

The train between South Bend and Chicago contains some interesting, if not always beautiful, sights. Although the train takes its name

20

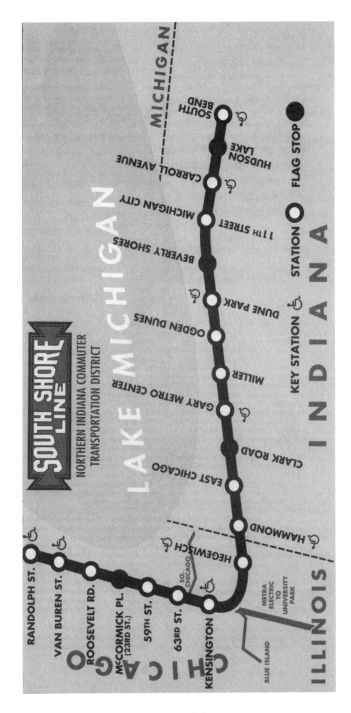

from Lake Michigan, that body of water is barely visible during the ride. Pretty Hudson Lake, just west of South Bend, is the most water that passengers get to see. Some of the smaller towns in Indiana have picturesque stations—be sure to see the Beverly Shores station, with its giant neon sign. In Gary, the train passes by US Steel's Gary Works, the largest steel mill in the world. Just before the ride ends at the Randolph Street Station, Soldier Field can be seen.

Randolph Street is in the heart of downtown Chicago. The Chicago Art Institute and the prime shopping along Michigan Avenue are within easy walking distance. The Field Museum of Natural History, the Shedd Aquarium, and the Museum of Science and Industry are best approached from one stop earlier, at Van Buren Street.

Visiting fans have long known of the South Shore's charms. For years, USC fans have stayed in a downtown Chicago hotel, and chartered a South Shore train to the game. Onboard, they are served a catered meal, and various forms of appropriate game day beverages. The University of Washington and Stanford have also chartered South Shore trains on game day. With the South Bend station moving to its current location, it is only a matter of time before more home fans discover the train, too.

AUTOMOBILES

Despite the charms of the train and the improvements at the airport, driving is still the most popular way to travel to South Bend. Motorists need to do some planning, though, especially with regard to the increasingly complicated parking situation.

From the South

Take I-65 north to Indianapolis. Take the 465 bypass around the city. Take the US 31 exit. US 31 takes you almost all the way to the campus. It is not an interstate, though, and some stretches are better than others. For example, travelling through Kokomo is very time consuming, with heavy traffic and plenty of traffic signals. Plan on the trip from Indianapolis to Notre Dame taking about three hours, in good weather.

Once in South Bend, follow the signs to stay on State Road 933—formerly US 33, and also called 31. This is the major road that divides the Notre Dame and St. Mary's campuses. You will see the Golden Dome on your right. If you are arriving on game day, continue north to Cleveland Road, then turn right. Turn right again, or south, onto Juniper. This will take you to the major general admission parking areas.

From the East or West

From the East or West, you will drive on I80/90—the Indiana Toll Road. The tolls are modest, and since South Bend is more or less centered in the state, you will pay roughly the same amount no matter which direction you are coming from—about $2. The drive from either the Ohio border or the Illinois border is about 90 miles.

Take exit 77, and proceed north on State Road 933, until you get to Cleveland Road. Turn right. Turn right on Juniper, and follow it to the major parking areas.

BANNED VEHICLES

As most Notre Dame alumni know, the university's administration has been waging a war on various forms of fun for decades. Sometimes, with the passage of time, we look back at this and laugh. Sometimes, though, it affects us in our present lives, and we remember what a pain the school's heavy hand can be. Such is the case with the school's ban on recreational vehicles.

The giant gas guzzling behemoths used to roll onto the campus days before the big games. Seeing them was as sure a sign of fall as the turning leaves. Driving a giant RV onto campus was seen by many as one of the goals of a Notre Dame education.

In 1993, after a memorably festive Florida State game, the university banned the overnight parking of RVs on campus property. Alumni, were, understandably, upset. The university claimed it was due to liability and security concerns. There are two problems with this reasoning. First, how come every other football school in America can somehow

23

manage to ignore this liability? Most schools, in fact, encourage tail-gating, with official events and local businesses sponsoring booths, tents, and music. The second falsehood is obvious to anyone who ever wit-nessed the RV legions at Notre Dame. The average age onboard was in the high double digits. While these people certainly did enjoy their tailgating, it is hard to imagine them as a threat to civil society. Inciden-tally, motorcycles are also banned on campus on game day—presum-ably some administrator saw someone having fun on one once.

While overnight parking is banned forever, RV owners can park their rigs on campus on game day, although no earlier than 7:45 AM. They must leave within three hours of the end of the game. As yet, the university has been unable to get fun banned statewide, so a cottage industry has sprung up near campus, with local homeowners renting their yards to recreational vehicles. It's not the same, though, as seeing hundreds of Airstreams, with Irish flags flying, lined up in silvery rows on Green Field.

PARKING

Notre Dame is a truly pedestrian campus. Students park only on huge lots at the periphery of the campus. The University prides itself on the large number of students who live on campus—there are no frater-nities or sororities at Notre Dame. The stadium is within walking dis-tance for all those who live on campus. Consequently, it is not until after graduation that students realize what a nightmare it is to find a parking spot on game day.

One of the immutable rules of Notre Dame football is that all the good spaces are reserved—this includes almost all of those that are ac-tually within sight of the stadium. These spaces belong to season ticket holders, major benefactors, and other varieties of big wigs. Green Field, formerly a tailgating Mecca, is now the DeBartolo Quad. Parking is also no longer allowed at Holy Cross College. The largest general admission parking lot is north of campus at Juniper and Pendle Roads. This lot has approximately 10,000 spaces, and costs $10 for the day. The price is reasonable, especially when you consider that it includes bus service to and from the stadium. The newly expanded stadium, though, holds 80,012 fans. About 10,000 of these are students, who don't need a parking space. If you figure an average of three to a car, the Juniper and Pendle lot will take care of about 30,000 more. This means that about half the stadium, 40,000 people, have to scramble for a spot.

There is only one relatively small public parking area south of the stadium, off of Angela. These spaces are also $10 for the day, but they are much better than the lot off of Juniper—they are actually within sight of the stadium. This lot is not a secret, though, so you have to get on campus pretty early to secure a space in this field.

The best advice is to avoid parking if at all possible. Almost all local hotels will offer some kind of transportation. South Bend city busses will pick up at all the hotels north of campus on State Road 31, and those hotels in Mishawaka. For information about this service, call 219-233-2131. If you must drive to the stadium, arrive early and try to park in the Pendle Lot.

When that lot fills up, your options dwindle. There is some limited public parking on the St. Mary's campus, which will be within reasonable walking distance of the stadium. Often these spaces are available until surprisingly late in the day. Enterprising homeowners around the edges of the campus will allow you to park on their lawns, usually for around $10.

GAME DAY TRAFFIC PATTERNS

Notre Dame and the local authorities have for years altered local traffic patterns on game day to facilitate traffic flow—it is an exercise in precision. At around 11:00 AM, for a 1:00 PM kickoff, all the roads surrounding the campus will be made one-way towards the campus. For about one hour after the game, all those roads are reversed, and are made one-way pointing away from campus.

A small army of officials, some of the unsung heroes of game day, enforces the patterns. These orange-vested myrmidons include not only the South Bend Police, but Indiana State Police, St. Joseph County

Police, Notre Dame Security, Civilian Volunteer Officers, Explorer Scouts, South Bend Traffic and Lighting, the St. Joseph County Highway Department, and the Indiana Toll Road commission. As you are driving to and from campus, you will see one of these people every 10 feet or so—follow their directions. They will get you where you're going, and anyway, you have no choice. There are many impressive sights at a Notre Dame home game. The martial effectiveness of the traffic control is surely among them.

A WORD ABOUT DAYLIGHT SAVINGS TIME

In Indiana, time can be confusing. This results from the confluence of two unusual circumstances. First, Indiana is divided into two time zones. The vast majority of the state is in the Eastern Time Zone, the same time zone as New York City—this includes Notre Dame. Five counties near Chicago, though, and five counties in the southern end of the state around Evansville, are in the Central Time Zone. The second cause of confusion is that Indiana is one of three states—the other two are Arizona and Hawaii—which does not observe Daylight Savings Time.

How does this affect you? For about the first two-thirds of the football season, Notre Dame is on the same time as Chicago. They are not in the same time zone, though—Chicago is on Central Daylight Time, while Notre Dame is on Eastern Standard Time. At 2:00 AM on the last Sunday of October, when the rest of the country "falls back," the time in Indiana stays the same. Now Notre Dame will have the same time as New York City, because they will both be on Eastern Standard Time. For the rest of the season, Notre Dame will be one hour ahead of Chicago.

Further adding to the confusion is that some counties in Indiana do observe Daylight Savings Time—five counties around Louisville and Cincinnati. Just remember that early in the season, Notre Dame has the same time as Chicago. Late in the season, they are on the same time as New York.

EVERYBODY'S TALKING ABOUT IT: THE WEATHER

Weather can be a big factor in planning your game day transportation. During the football season, the average temperature drops from 71F in August to 41F in November. South Bend's famous "lake effect" snow can affect transportation as well. Some facts and figures:

—AVERAGE NOTRE DAME TEMPERATURES—

	Jan	Feb	Mar	Apr	May	Jun	Jul	Aug	Sept	Oct	Nov	Dec
Ave. High	30	34	46	59	70	79	83	81	74	62	48	35
Ave.	23	26	37	49	59	69	73	71	64	53	41	29
Ave. Low	16	19	29	39	49	59	63	61	54	43	33	22

Football Season

Nothing brings modern transportation to a grinding halt like snow. South Bend gets its share—an average of 71 inches a year. The majority of this is "lake effect" snow. This atmospheric phenomenon results when cold Arctic air sucks up moisture over the Great Lakes, and then dumps it on the lee side landfall. The results can be impressive: residents of the Tug Hill Plateau in New York get 300 inches of snow a year from the lake effect. Luckily for fans, South Bend is not hit nearly that hard.

—AVERAGE NOTRE DAME SNOWFALL—-

	Jan	Feb	Mar	Apr	May	Jun	Jul	Aug	Sept	Oct	Nov	Dec
In.	19	15	9	2	0	0	0	0	0	1	8	18

                                          └—— Football Season ——┘

FOR VERY, VERY SUCCESSFUL FANS

You can fly your private jet to the game—75 to 100 private aircraft fly in every weekend. The record is 185 planes, all of which flew in for the 1993 Florida State game—the same game that earned recreational vehicles a lifetime ban on university property.

Private fliers land on Bendix field, which is part of Michiana Regional Airport. Logistics are managed by Corporate Wings, whose number is 219-233-8285.

To rent a small corporate jet for the weekend, with pilot, costs about $1,500 per hour. If you have to ask . . .

Numbers you should know: 1928

The Gipper

"I've got to go, Rock. It's all right. I'm not afraid. Some time, Rock, when the team is up against it, when things are going wrong and the breaks are beating the boys—tell them to go in there with all they've got and win just one for the Gipper. I don't know where I'll be then, Rock. But I'll know about it, and I'll be happy."
—George Gipp, 1920

"The day before he died, George Gipp asked me to wait until the situation seemed hopeless—then ask a Notre Dame team to go out and beat Army for him. This is the day, and you are the team."—Knute Rockne, November 10, 1928

George Gipp was born in 1895 in Laurium, Michigan. He went to Notre Dame to play baseball, but was spotted by Rockne casually kicking footballs across the quad, and the rest is history. During his career, the Irish went 27-2-3. George Gipp was named Notre Dame's first All-American in 1920. Two weeks later, he contracted strep throat, made his famous deathbed request, and died.

Eight years later, Rockne made his speech to a embattled Notre Dame team at halftime. The Irish had lost twice that season, and were facing an unbeaten Army team in Yankee Stadium. After Rockne's speech, the inspired Irish beat Army, 12-6.

Amazingly, 80 years after his death, George Gipp still holds some team records at Notre Dame:
- Rushing yards per attempt, season: 8.1 yards per carry, 1920
- Total offensive yards per attempt, season: 9.37, 1920

- Kickoff returns in a game: 8 for 157 yards against Army, 1920
- Total kick returns in a game: 10 for 207 yards against Army, 1920
- Gipp's record for career rushing—2,341 yards—stood for over 50 years, until it was broken by Jerome Heavens in 1978.

Photo courtesy of the University of Notre Dame Photography Department

Chapter Four

FROM THE CONCIERGE FLOOR TO THE DORM ROOM FLOOR: Lodging

DON'T LOOK FOR A STATELY row of fraternity houses at Notre Dame—there aren't any. Sororities, either. Fraternities have never been chartered by the university, as they were long ago deemed inconsistent with the school's educational and spiritual missions. Students live in the same dorm for their entire four-year stay. None of the dorms are co-ed. This unusual system results in lifelong friendships, and a lifelong loyalty to the residence halls, which house more than 75 percent of Notre Dame's students. All those students are blissfully unaware of how valuable their rooms are until graduation—they spend four football seasons at Notre Dame within walking distance of the stadium.

While a recent hotel construction boom in Mishawaka has eased the pain somewhat, getting a room for the big game is harder than ever—remember, the stadium now holds 80,012 fans. Even with the construction boom, there are still only 3,560 rooms in all of St. Joseph County. Needless to stay, the law of supply and demand applies, so you can expect to pay a premium at any area hotel for a game weekend. The closer you get to the stadium, the more you will pay.

Unless otherwise noted, every hotel listed here requires a two-night stay. Some require those two nights to be Friday and Saturday; others allow you to stay any two consecutive nights. Ask for details when you make your reservation.

The "Availability" ranking is based on inquiries made during the summer, for the upcoming season. Many hotels will not allow you to make reservations more than one year a head of time, and, unless you are a season ticket holder, you won't know for which games you have tickets that far ahead of time, anyway. This ranking presumes that most fans make their football plans during the summer. Just as with airline tickets, though, sometimes you can slip into a vacancy by waiting until the last minute. All the hotels have waiting lists for booked football weekends, as well. All rates given apply to game weekends only.

WALKING DISTANCE

MORRIS INN
Notre Dame Avenue • 219-631-2000 • 92 Rooms
Game Day Rates: Not Applicable • Availability: None

The university's official hotel has some fancy-pants pretensions that can be annoying—it is really little more than a dorm with a cash bar. It is, however, in an ideal location, almost equidistant from the stadium and the Golden Dome. Don't plan on staying there on a game weekend, though—the university's trustees reserve the hotel in its entirety for every football weekend.

For several years, rumors have abounded about plans for a new

Morris Inn. Certainly, standards have changed since the hotel opened 50 years ago. The university is also keen to improve its convention and conference facilities. In fact, a location has already been staked out for the new hotel—it will move about one block down Notre Dame Avenue, where it will share a parking lot with the new bookstore. For now, though, despite the rumors, no timetable exists for building the new Morris Inn.

The hotel is part of Notre Dame lore. It was built in 1950, the result of a one million-dollar gift from Ernest Morris, a 1906 Notre Dame Law School graduate. He went on to become a fabulously successful South Bend businessman, and he was always grateful to Notre Dame for his education. For us non-big wigs, the hotel does offer some nice packages for the off-season. For most football fans, though, the Morris Inn might as well be located on the moon.

JAMISON INN
1404 North Ivy Road • 219-277-9682 • 49 Rooms
Game Day Rates: $200-$225 per night • Availability: None

This sophisticated and comfortable hotel is located just southeast of the stadium. While its location is less central than the Morris Inn's, it

33

is actually closer to the stadium. Your odds of getting a room are slightly better, as well.

Owners Pat McGraw and Jim Musuraca built the Jamison Inn in 1986. Those names might sound familiar to Irish fans—they played football at Notre Dame from 1970 to 1972. It's one of those ideas so good you wonder why no one thought of it sooner—buy a parcel of land as close as you can to Notre Dame Stadium and build a hotel. The hotel is independent of the university, but the two entities have a cozy relationship. For example: during the holidays, when the dorms close, the basketball team stays at the Jamison Inn.

When you see the Jamison Inn, you may think that it looks bigger than 49 rooms. It is, but most of the Jamison Inn is made up of condos. These rooms are obviously unavailable to the general publics.

As for those other 49 rooms—your odds are probably better if you call a week before the game than if you call a year before. The hotel management keeps close control of the game day rooms, but they do allow the occasional regular joe through the door. There are no tricks— just call, get your name on the waiting list, and hope for a minor miracle. Don't bother with a sob story. General Manager Janice Bella says that often she gets calls from old alumni who say they will be coming to their "last game," and that they would like to stay at the Jamison Inn. She says with a chuckle that such stories no longer affect her.

The hotel's extremely comfortable dining room hosts most of its game-related activities. On Friday night, they host a happy hour. On Saturday mornings, they send you off with a hearty breakfast. The hotel also hosts a post-game tailgater with cocktails and snacks.

THE INN AT ST. MARY'S
53993 US 31/33 North • 800-94STMARY • 150 Rooms
Game Day Rates: $209-$215 per night • Availability: Very Little

This is the newest of the walking-distance hotels, and in many ways the best. Like the Morris Inn, it is university-owned, and has a slightly

utilitarian outside appearance. Unlike the Morris Inn, the Inn at St. Mary's redeems itself inside with a beautiful atrium lobby, and comfortable, modern rooms. Also unlike the Morris Inn, you have at least an outside shot at a game day room at St. Mary's.

The hotel was built in 1992, with 120 rooms. It was an immediate success, so the hotel added 30 rooms in 1997. The hotel has no restaurant, but does serve breakfast every day. St. Mary's students make up most of the hotel's desk staff.

The Inn at St. Mary's has an unusual waiting list. Once you get a room, you are given first crack at the room for the same game next year. In other words, if you get a room for the second home game this year, you are guaranteed the room for the second home game next year, if you want it. This means that once you get in the system, you could potentially have a room within walking distance of the stadium for the rest of your life.

About that distance—the Inn at St. Mary's is about two miles from the stadium—the very edge of what this book considers walking distance. While the hotel does have shuttle service, most people prefer the 30-minute stroll.

HIGHWAY 31

For years, the section of Highway 31 north of campus was hotel row for Notre Dame fans. There are 10 hotels between the toll road exit

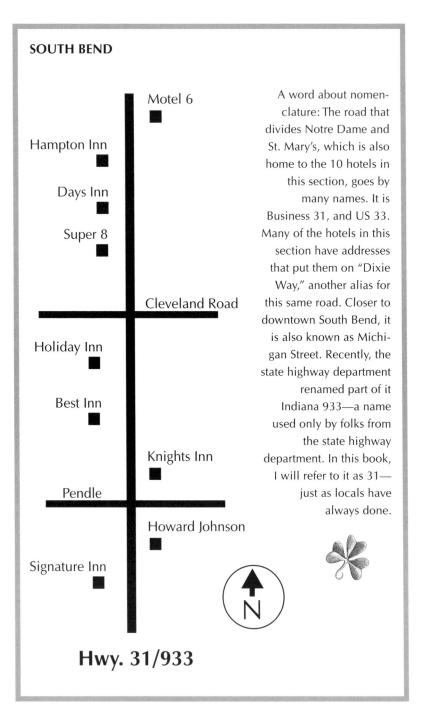

Motel 6

Hampton Inn

Days Inn

Super 8

Cleveland Road

Holiday Inn

Best Inn

Knights Inn

Pendle

Howard Johnson

Signature Inn

A word about nomenclature: The road that divides Notre Dame and St. Mary's, which is also home to the 10 hotels in this section, goes by many names. It is Business 31, and US 33. Many of the hotels in this section have addresses that put them on "Dixie Way," another alias for this same road. Closer to downtown South Bend, it is also known as Michigan Street. Recently, the state highway department renamed part of it Indiana 933—a name used only by folks from the state highway department. In this book, I will refer to it as 31— just as locals have always done.

N

Hwy. 31/933

and the Michigan border—the furthest is only 3.1 miles from the stadium. While a recent spate of hotel building in Mishawaka has reduced its status somewhat, many a Notre Dame fan still finds a room among this group of chain hotels. The hotels are listed in order of their proximity to the campus.

Some of the hotels along 31 bill themselves as being within walking distance of the stadium. For most of us, though, city busses provide the best transportation. For $5, you will be taken directly to the stadium, and returned to your hotel.

SIGNATURE INN
215 Dixie Way South • 800-822-5252 • 123 Rooms
$165 per night • Availability: Some

The Signature Inn is the hotel on 31 closest to the campus. It is also one of the newer ones, giving it a nicer feel than some of its older neighbors. The Signature Inn holds a unique distinction—it hosts the university VIPs who don't fit in the Morris Inn. The hotel's management downplays this, but it is a telling endorsement.

The hotel has a waiting list very similar to the one at the Inn at St. Mary's. Guests during football weekends get the first shot at reserving those rooms for the same game the following year.

HOWARD JOHNSON INN
130 Dixie Way South • 800-348-2412 • 132 Rooms
$150 per night • Availability: Some

Formerly known as the Randall Inn, the Hojo is something of a landmark. Since the name-change, the hotel has greatly improved its appearance. The hotel has a pool that is immediately adjacent to a glass wall in its restaurant, making both swimmers and eaters somewhat self-conscious.

The Hojo is one of few hotels in the area that allows reservations more than one year a head of time. In fact there is no limit—you can reserve your room now for the 2002 Rutgers game, if you like.

KNIGHTS INN
236 Dixie Way South • 219-277-2960 • 108 Rooms
$149 per night • Availability: Some

Most of the hotels along 31 have undergone several renovations in their history, which is the kind of gentrification that some people bemoan in America. If you feel that we have become too soft, and are looking for a truly seedy lodging experience, then the Knights Inn is for you. While the chain has done away with the purple sheets that used to be a Knights Inn trademark, it is still a throwback to the days when you never needed to be reminded to lock your door with the chain. The hotel has a football weekend reservation "contract."

BEST INN
425 Dixie Way North • 219-277-7700 • 93 rooms
$110 per night • Availability: Very Little

Every football season for 10 years, the Best Inn has called the same people, and given them the first crack at reservations for the next year's football season. The staff will tell you candidly that if you are not on that list, you will not be getting on. The good news is that these loyal customers do not fill the hotel. As you might have guessed, there is a procedure for getting one of those other rooms.

Call at noon, on February 6. The hotel takes reservations on its remaining rooms on this day every year, and sells out in around 15 minutes.

HOLIDAY INN
University Area • 515 Dixie Way North • 219-272-6600
228 Rooms • $200-$250 per night • Availability: Very Little

This is the kind of Holiday Inn that used to proudly advertise its "Holidome": a recreation area with a pool, miniature golf, video games, ping pong, and South Bend's only regulation shuffleboard court. At some point about 10 years ago, though, some marketing genius at Holiday

Inn Corporate must have decided that Holidomes were too corny for America in the 1990s—you'll recall that that's about the same time they got rid of their famous lighted signs. They no longer proudly advertise those select Holiday Inns that have achieved Holidome status. Despite that, the Holidome is still there, it is still fun, and this is still one of my favorite hotels in the area.

In addition to the Holidome, the hotel hosts many more game-related activities than its Highway 31 neighbors do. Every game weekend, they host a tailgater party. They also have an outdoor barbecue with a champagne fountain. The Holiday Inn is also home to the Gipper's Lounge, and the Gipper's Café, two Notre Dame-themed restaurants.

RAMADA INN
52890 US 31 North • 219-272-5220 • 203 Rooms
$150 per night • Availability: Some

Like the nearby Holiday Inn, the Ramada has some amenities than can make for a particularly enjoyable weekend—a very nice pool area, a putting green, a game room, and a lounge. Mitigating these nice features, though, is the most Byzantine reservation procedure of any hotel in South Bend.

Reservation applications for football weekends must be made in writing, only—no phone calls on the subject will be accepted. Payment must be made by cash or check—no credit cards will be accepted on game weekends. Is the Ramada Inn protesting our credit card culture? Or are they part of some bizarre shadow government that is financing illicit arms sales through the cash it gathers during game weekends? No one at the hotel is willing to explain this policy. Call the above number for detailed instructions on how to make your reservation request.

SUPER 8
52825 US 31/33 North • 219-272-9000 • 111 Rooms
$125 per night • Availability: Good

Life's Great at the Super 8—Except for the Really High Rate. One-hundred-twenty-five dollars per night is not really that high, unless you take into consideration the near total absence of amenities. Maybe because of this, the hotel does have an unusual number of rooms available for game weekends.

DAYS INN
52757 US 31 North • 219-277-0510 • 180 Rooms
$179 per night • Availability: Some

This rate shames even the neighboring Super 8. While the hotel is undergoing a major renovation, it will have to be one spectacular overhaul to justify $179. There is absolutely no way they should charge more than the exponentially nicer Hampton Inn, which also happens to be brand new, and is right next door. There is no greater testament to the economic power of ND football than the fact that this hotel will probably sell out for every game.

HAMPTON INN & SUITES
52709 US 31 North • 219-279-9373 • 109 Rooms
$175 per night • Availability: Very Little

This is a nice, new hotel with (relatively speaking) reasonable rates. Consequently, it sells out in a hurry. In one day, as a matter of fact.

Every year, the hotel picks one day in early December to open up the reservations for the upcoming season. On that day, starting at 10:00 AM Eastern Standard Time, you must call the chain's central reservation desk at 1-800-426-7866. Calls to the hotel itself, or even a personal visit to the hotel, will be futile.

If you are lucky enough to get a room, you must, within 30 days, forward a deposit in the form of a check or money order. Any cancellations within 60 days of the game will result in forfeiting the deposit.

MOTEL 6
52624 US 31 North • 219-272-7072 • 146 Rooms
$85.99 per night • Availability: Very Good

This is the hotel furthest north on Highway 31—it is only 2.5 miles from the Michigan border. Even so, it is still only 3.1 miles from the stadium. It is also one of the best deals in town.

Motel 6 is the only hotel on 31 that does not require a two-night stay. It also has the lowest game day rate of any hotel on 31, by a significant margin. Chain-wide, Motel 6 has worked hard to overcome its fleabag image, and this hotel is a beneficiary of that new philosophy. It is brand new, clean, relatively spacious, and even has a pool. It also has more rooms available for football weekends than any other hotel on 31.

MISHAWAKA

St. Joseph County is one of the fastest growing counties in Indiana. South Bend, the county's biggest city, is not seeing this growth—its population is actually dropping. In fact, the population of South Bend recently dropped below 100,000 for the first time in over 50 years. The population growth is occurring in neighboring communities—especially Mishawaka.

Most Notre Dame students know Mishawaka from the University Park Mall. The mall area, in fact, has been the cornerstone of Mishawaka's economic growth. Mishawaka, though, is not a bedroom community for South Bend, but a vibrant, historic community in its own right. It is east of South Bend, adjacent to it along the St. Joseph River. The University Park area is in the northwestern corner of the city. Mishawaka's population is 50,000—about half that of South Bend's.

The number of hotel rooms in Mishawaka has risen dramatically in the last five years. The city now boasts nine hotels, with a total of 800 rooms. While this represents just about 20 percent of the county's total rooms, it represents the majority of new rooms. Notre Dame fans should note, too, that new hotels often have surprisingly high availability, because they have not made it onto the lists of many returning fans.

VARSITY CLUBS OF AMERICA
3800 North Main St. • 800-946-4822 • 60 Rooms
$175 per night • Availability: Very Little

This hotel is the new Mecca for visiting Notre Dame fans. It displays the largest off-campus collection of Notre Dame memorabilia. The lobby has theater-sized television screens that play ND highlights continuously, alongside a 24-hour sports ticker. The breakfast buffet is called the Touchdown Buffet, and the restaurant is the Stadium Sports Grill. Even the swing set outside is painted blue and gold. On Saturday mornings, South Bend radio legend Bob Lux broadcasts his pre-game show from the hotel's lobby, insuring frequent sightings of Notre Dame

Author Todd Tucker talks with radio personality Bob Lux at the Varsity Clubs of America.

celebrities. Nowhere, not even at the Morris Inn, will a Notre Dame fan feel more at home. Even if you don't get a room, you should come into the lobby, as good a shrine to Irish football as you will see.

And, you probably won't get a room. Like the Jamison Inn, the VCA sells a large number of its rooms as condominiums. It has a relatively small number of rooms to begin with, so you can see that the odds are against you. Your best bet is to check at the desk on Friday night or Saturday morning for a last-minute cancellation.

STUDIO PLUS
4715 North Main St. • 219-255-8031 • 72 Rooms
$129 per night • Availability: Some

This is another property whose mission is not really geared to the weekend fan. It is an extended-stay facility, designed for executives in transition and the like. Each room is really an apartment, complete with a kitchen and living area. They won't even take reservations. However, if you show up on game day, you can check at the desk, and they will rent you a room if available. You will get just about the biggest room in town, at a very reasonable rate, if you are willing to take that chance.

COURTYARD BY MARRIOTT
4825 N. Main Street • 219-273-9900 • 78 Rooms
$179-$225 per night • Availability: Very Little

This new hotel is booked solid very early on, indicative of the quality rooms and the reasonable price. They have a standard waiting list for those who are shut out.

BEST WESTERN
5640 North Main St. • 219-247-4000 • 73 Rooms
$140 per night • Availability: Very Good

This is the newest of the nine hotels in northern Mishawaka—they opened their doors in July 1999. Of the 73 rooms, 20 are suites with kitchens, and eight are spa rooms with a whirlpool bath. Best of all, because they are so new, the hotel has rooms available for almost every game until very late in the summer.

HOLIDAY INN EXPRESS
6701 North Main Street • 219-271-1700 • 62 Rooms
$175-300 per night • Availability: Very Good

This hotel is only four years old, but it still has a surprising number of rooms available. It is also conveniently located near the mall, theaters, and many restaurants. This is good, because like every other Holiday Inn Express, they have no restaurant of their own. They do have an indoor pool, though.

CARLTON LODGE
420 West University Drive • 219-277-2520 • 80 Rooms
$225 per night • Availability: Very Good

When asked in July, the Carlton had rooms available for every single upcoming game. This may be a reflection of their prices, which are slightly higher than their neighbors. The hotel attempts to have a lodge-feel throughout, with limited success. The Carlton Lodge and the neighboring Holiday Inn Express are owned by the same folks.

THE FAIRFIELD INN
425 University Drive • 219-273-2202 • 62 Rooms
$150 per night • Availability: Very Little

The Fairfield chain is a lower-price spin-off of Marriott. They have a large variety of amenities, though, including a free continental breakfast and an indoor pool and spa. With all this at $150, you can see why this hotel sells out so quickly. Incidentally, this hotel is owned by the same management group that runs the nearby Hampton Inn.

HAMPTON INN
445 University Drive • 219-273-2309 • 63 Rooms
$150-$175 per night • Availability: Very Little

Indoor pool, spa, free "deluxe" continental breakfast, free local calls, in-room coffeemakers, irons and ironing boards, so that you can iron the wrinkles out of your plaid pants before heading to the game. Reservations are not taken until the last game of the season.

SUPER 8
535 W. University Drive • 219-247-0888 • 66 Rooms
$129 per night • Availability: Very Little

While this is definitely a no frills operation, this Super 8 is brand new, making the rooms clean and comfortable. Notice their rate—they are about the same price as their evil cousin on 31, but this newer property is infinitely more pleasant.

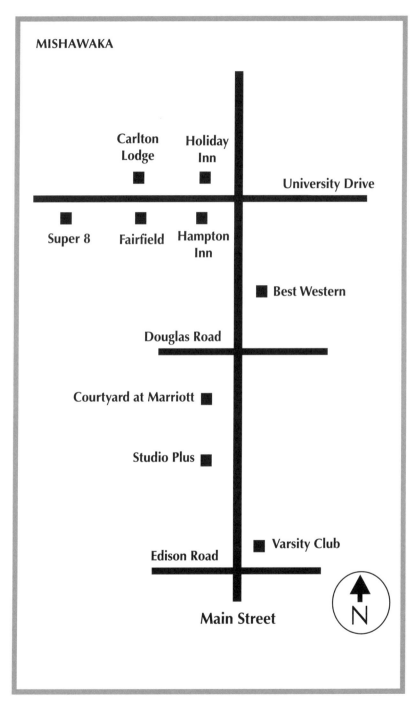

MISHAWAKA

Carlton Lodge

Holiday Inn

University Drive

Super 8   Fairfield   Hampton Inn

Best Western

Douglas Road

Courtyard at Marriott

Studio Plus

Varsity Club

Edison Road

Main Street

N

DOWNTOWN SOUTH BEND

Downtown lodging is a study in contrasts. You can choose from high-rise executive-type hotels, including South Bend's largest, or a five-room bed & breakfast. The downtown area, in fact, is home to three very nice B&Bs, all three of which are located along a quiet stretch of West Washington Street.

THE MARRIOTT
123 N. St. Joseph Street • 219-234-2000 • 299 rooms
$259 per night • Availability: Very Good

South Bend's largest hotel is also home to the best game day availability in the city. An inquiry made in July revealed that the hotel had rooms available for every single upcoming game. No doubt this has something to do with the hefty price tag. If money is no object, though, the Marriott has a lot to offer. It is home to two restaurants: Allie's American Grill and Tokyo, a Benihana-style Japanese restaurant. The hotel has an impressive pool area, and a spectacular enclosed lobby that it shares with First Source Bank. Also of note to fans is that the hotel is directly across the street from the College Football Hall of Fame.

THE HOLIDAY INN DOWNTOWN
213 West Washington St. • 219-232-3941 • 177 rooms
$239 per night • Availability: Some

This 16-story hotel has suffered from neglect in the recent past. New management, though, has just completed a $2.5 million renovation, and the results of their efforts are obvious in every room.

Like the Marriott, the hotel is geared more for business travelers than for football loving families—it has a somewhat cold personality. The renovation did add a pool, though, and the restaurant, Platters, is comfortable. Also like the Marriott, the hotel had a large number of rooms available two months before the season started.

THE QUEEN ANNE INN BED & BREAKFAST
420 West Washington • 800-582-2379 • 6 rooms
$150-$200 per night • Hosts: Bob and Pauline Medhurst
Availability: Very Little

As is the case with many B&Bs, the rooms here are themed. In this case, they are all named for birds: the Bluebird Room, the Scarlet Tanager Room, The Oriole Room, etc. All the rooms have private baths, and one even hides an ancient wall safe behind a mirror. The owners won't turn children away, but they certainly don't welcome them—their brochure advertises the "limited activities available" for the little tykes. You probably won't have to choose between your children and a room at the Queen Anne Inn, anyway: their waiting list is currently over four years long.

THE BOOK INN

508 West Washington • 219-288-1990 • 5 rooms • $150-$190 per
night • Availability: Good • Hosts: John and Peggy Livingston

For some reason, this B&B, only one block away from the Queen
Anne, has rooms available for almost every game. In this case, the theme
is literary—every room is named for an author, such as Emily Dickinson.
The theme is more than window dressing—owner Peggy runs an excel-
lent used bookstore in the basement.

The Book Inn has some notable common areas, including a roomy
front porch with plenty of swings. Among the other nice touches are

Waterford Crystal at breakfast, and fresh flowers in your room every morning.

THE OLIVER INN BED AND BREAKFAST
630 West Washington • 219-232-4545 • 9 rooms • $137-199 per night
Availability: Some • Hosts: Richard and Venera Monohan

The most inviting of the three B&Bs in every way, right down to the gracious hostess. The numerous board games in the living room make it look like some actual living goes on there. A gorgeous baby grand piano provides live music at breakfast. A "Butler's Pantry" provides free snacks for those of us who cannot always schedule our hunger. The Oliver Inn is on a larger lot than the others, as well—a full acre. This contributes greatly to its high overall comfort level.

OUTLYING AREAS

Fans who can tolerate a little bit of a drive will be rewarded with lower rates and increased availability. Each of the cities listed below is within 45 minutes of the campus, and each is used to seeing football fans on fall Saturday mornings.

PLYMOUTH: Thirty miles south of campus on Highway 31. In recent years, the city has become something of a lodging center—most of the hotels are relatively new. The following hotels are available in Plymouth:

DAYS INN
219-935-4276
36 Rooms
SUPER 8
219-936-8856
59 Rooms
MOTEL 6
219-935-5911
103 Rooms
HOLIDAY INN
219-936-4013
108 Rooms
Note: This Holiday Inn is where the Notre Dame team spends the night before home games.

ELKHART: Thirty miles east of campus on US 20, or I-80/90. Elkhart is home to eight RV factories, and the RV Hall of Fame. Despite their love affair with mobile living, though, they do have a variety of hotels:

DAYS INN
219-262-3541
122 Rooms
HAMPTON INN
219-264-2525
62 Rooms
KNIGHTS INN
219-264-4262
118 Rooms

SUPER 8
219-264-4457
62 Rooms
HOLIDAY INN EXPRESS
219-262-0014
62 Rooms

CAMPGROUNDS

Indiana is the recreational vehicle capital of the world. The RV was invented in Indiana, the world's largest RV showroom is in Richmond, Indiana, and more manufacturers of RVs (18) are located in Indiana than in any other state. The International Recreational Vehicle Museum and Hall of Fame is located in Elkhart, Indiana, just east of Mishawaka. Except for the fatwa the University of Notre Dame issued on RVs in 1993, there is no better place in the world to visit in your recreational vehicle. Just don't bring it on campus before 7:45 AM on game day.

SOUTH BEND EAST KOA
50707 Princess Way • Granger, Indiana 46530 • 219-277-1335
Rate for two adults in an RV with full hook-ups: $24.95

The closest campground to campus, this KOA features 50-amp hook-ups, laundry, showers, swimming, and free movies. Tent campers are also welcome. This is the only campground close enough to the campus to occasionally sell out for game weekends. Even so, the campground does not raise its rates for football weekends. The campground closes for the season on November 20, so it may not be available for that last game.

EBY'S PINES CAMPGROUND
14583 SR 120
Bristol, Indiana 46507
219-848-4583
Rate for two adults in an RV with full hook-ups: $20.90

Although 45 minutes from campus, this campground's deluxe facilities make it worth considering: two pools, a laundry, a store complete with video rentals, game room, fishing, and even a roller skating rink. Probably because of its distance, the campground sees almost no visible increase in business during game weekends, and it never sells out. The campground closes for the season on October 15.

ELKHART COUNTY/MIDDLEBURY EXIT KOA
52867 SR 13
Middlebury, Indiana 46540
219-825-5932
Rates for two adults in an RV with full hook-ups: $23.95

Cabins, free movies, 50-amp hook-ups, hiking trail, miniature golf, playground, propane sales, petting zoo, and a store. Also arranges RV plant tours at a nearby factory. Like Eby's Pines, this campground sees no noticeable increase in business during game weekends. Closes for the season on October 31. Thirty miles east of the ND exit on I80/90.

A FINAL WORD ABOUT THE RESIDENCE HALLS

Each dorm at Notre Dame is headed by a rector, who is usually a priest or a nun. Like the captain of a ship, the rector has tremendous power to run his or her dorm. Most of the rules regarding overnight guests are at the discretion of the rector, and are unique to each hall. One thing you can be sure of, though, is that overnight-intergender-comingling of any sort is strictly prohibited.

Many colleges have rules similar to Notre Dame, whereby visitors of the opposite sex are prohibited from staying overnight in a dorm room. At Notre Dame, these rules are more than mere formality. They are strictly enforced, and they are enforced in every dorm, whether male or female. Remember—there are no coed dorms at Notre Dame. Students can and do get thrown out of school for violating this rule, so don't bother asking.

If you have a friend on campus, though, and you happen to be of the same gender, perhaps you can find a ragged recliner in their room to sleep upon, or a sticky corner of dorm-room floor. Make sure they get permission from the rector ahead of time, and enjoy your authentic Notre Dame experience. If you start to feel that the gritty realities of dormitory living are beneath you, remember—the rooms are pretty much the same at the Morris Inn.

Cavanaugh Hall

Numbers you should know: 0-0

The 1946 Army Game

Coach Frank Leahy was away from Notre Dame for two years during World War II. During those two years, Army crushed Notre Dame: 59-0 in 1944, and 48-0 in 1945. Those defeats were much on the mind of Leahy when he returned to his head-coaching job. He made his "lads" chant in practice: "Fifty-nine and forty-eight, this is the year we retaliate."

The November 9, 1946, game would be played in Yankee Stadium—it had been sold out since June. The Cadets had won 25 straight games, and had in their offense the two most famous players Army would ever have—Mr. Inside and Mr. Outside, Doc Blanchard and Glen Davis. Both men would go on to win the Heisman. Notre Dame had a future Heisman winner on the field as well, in Johnny Lujack.

Both teams played extremely cautiously, the play-calling seemingly affected by the tremendous hype that surrounded the game. Army came close to scoring only once, near the end of the game. Doc Blanchard crossed into Notre Dame territory for the first time that day, and broke into the open field. Only a shoestring tackle on the 37-yard line prevented him from scoring, and preserved the tie. That tackle was made by none other than Johnny Lujack, who would win the Heisman the next year primarily for his exploits as quarterback. The biggest play of his career, though, may have been a tackle.

Just as in 1966, Notre Dame won the 1946 National Championship with a tie blemishing its record. The Irish finished the season 8-0-1. It was the first of four straight seasons that Leahy would coach without a loss.

(Recommended reading: ***LEAHY'S LADS: The Story of the Famous Notre Dame Football Teams of the 1940s*** by Jack Connor. Published by Diamond Communications, Inc., of South Bend, Indiana and available through the Notre Dame Bookstore.)

Notre Dame National Champions of 1946

First row: Livingstone, Rovai, Skogland, Kosikowski, Brown, Zmijewski, Cifelli, Russell, Mello, Angnone, Fischer, and Strohmeyer. Second row: Coutre, Hart, McGee, J. Brennan, Gompers, T. Brennan, McBride, Urban, Signaigo, Scott, Smith, Heywood, and Espenan. Third row: Wightkin, Zilly, Limont, Wm. Walsh, Connor, Ciatt, Meter, McGurk, Ashbaugh, Lujack, Fallon, Earley, LeCluyse. Fourth row: Zalejski, Sullivan, Mastrangelo, Brutz, Simmons, Potter, Tobin, Wendell, R. Walsh, O'Connor, and Ratterman. Fifth row: Martin, Czarobski, McGehee, Swistowicz, Panelli, Cowhig, Statuto, and Mgrs. Boss, Flaherty, Earls, and Kelly.

Photo courtesy of the University of Notre Dame Photography Department

Chapter Five

NEW MUSEUM PROVES OTHER TEAMS EXIST:
The College Football Hall of Fame

MOVING THE COLLEGE Football Hall of Fame from King's Island, Ohio, to South Bend in 1995 was one of the least controversial decisions in the history of South Bend City government. After all, the Rock and Roll Hall of Fame had recently resurrected Cleveland, another rusty post-industrial city. The College Football Hall of Fame had lined up some impressive corporate sponsors, including Coca-Cola, the US Postal Service, Alka Seltzer, and Burger King. Best of all, the hall was guaranteed that for at least six weekends a year, the hotels and motels of northern Indiana would be packed with rabid college football fans. It seemed like an idea that couldn't miss. Mayor Joe Kernan, now the lieutenant governor of Indiana, said they would attract 200,000 patrons a year to the hall, "in our sleep." It hasn't exactly worked out that way.

The hall has been losing money since it moved to South Bend, and taxpayers have been left holding the bag. They were promised that the hall would be a tourist magnet, but big crowds have never materialized. Especially disappointing has been the lack of a spillover from Notre Dame games. The Fridays before home games are still the hall's busiest days, but the crowd rarely gets above 1,000. When you consider that a sold-out Notre Dame Stadium now holds 80,012 dedicated football fans, you can understand why the hall's organizers are

frustrated. Taxpayers were frustrated, too, that the tourist magnet turned out to be a money pit. Coca-Cola and Burger King ended their sponsorships, and no big names stepped in to replace them. The Hall of Fame became a source of angry debate at City Council meetings. For a while, the hall's future in South Bend appeared to be in jeopardy.

The hall has responded by stepping up its marketing efforts on all fronts. They hired a full-time marketing manager. The hall and a national marketing firm, Host Communications, formed a strategic alliance. Ads aimed at Notre Dame fans—"Everybody Plays!"—are now everywhere on game day. On the Fridays before home games, there is a free shuttle that operates between Notre Dame's main circle and the hall—the trip is about 10 minutes, one-way. The hall now has an exhibit that features ND's latest opponent. Visiting marching bands play a concert on the hall's Astroturf field on the Friday before a game.

Bernie Kish, the hall's executive director, has also carefully reached out to South Bend's disgruntled citizenry. He invited all the locals to see the museum for free one day in 1998. He also permanently reduced the admission fee for residents of St. Joseph County. Attendance has never approached Mayor Kernan's 200,000—the best year was 1996, the hall's first, when 88,154 people came through the turnstiles. In the year 2000 Mayor Steve Luecke and the City Council bit the bullet and raised property taxes to pay for the hall and its operating deficit. To say that this was an unpopular rescue is putting it mildly.

As for Notre Dame fans, we are famous traditionalists, so it has taken some time for the new hall to become incorporated into the fan's routine. Fans are catching on, though: the College Football Hall of Fame is the perfect side trip during a football weekend.

The hall is located at 111 South St. Joseph Street, in the heart of downtown South Bend. Look for the striking glass and steel Marriott— the hall is across the street from it. The hall is a striking building in its own right. It is designed to look from the outside like half of a stadium, which embraces 25 yards of an Astroturf field, including the goalposts. The hall as a whole is enormously sensitive to college football tradition, so one has to wonder how they could cover their front lawn with Astroturf. Anyway, this field is where the hall's inductees usually play a game of flag football during the annual "Enshrinement Weekend." It is also where the visiting marching bands play their Friday afternoon concerts.

Not every school's marching band travels with the team to South

Bend. Notre Dame's band, for example, usually travels to only one away game per year, plus any bowl game. Because of Notre Dame's unique status, though, a large number of schools do send their bands. USC, Michigan, Purdue, Navy, and Michigan State always send their bands to Notre Dame.

When you walk into the hall, the gift shop is to your left, and Jersey Mikes and Scoops Ice Cream are to the right. The ticket counter is dead ahead. After paying, you walk down a spiraling ramp, which surrounds the sculpture that dominates the hall's atrium: "The Pursuit of the Dream."

The sculpture provides the first impression of the hall, which is unfortunate. It is the hall's greatest weak point. It is supposed to depict the progression of a football player from elementary school to college. In fact, it is incoherent, and obnoxiously modern. Stacks of pizza and detergent boxes, for example, form an inexplicably large part of the sculpture. The names of some college football greats are stenciled on the sculpture's lockers. This is the artist's sole reference to specific college football luminaries. Walk briskly down the ramp, and into the museum, and try not to hold a grudge against this victory of form over substance. Better things await you inside. Some highlights:

THE STADIUM THEATER—Without question, this movie is the best thing in the hall. You can sit in the bleachers, or, take it from me, on the player's bench. Watch as the bleachers depicted on the eight screens that surround you fill gradually with fans. This "pre-game" portion of the movie lasts 10 minutes.

The main film is a 13-minute distillation of a college football game, from the pre-game pep talk, to kickoff, to the half-time show, to the victory celebration. Throughout the movie, the filmmakers show great knowledge of the game in the scenes and teams that they select. For instance, Eddie Robinson, in his last season at Grambling, gives his team a pre-game pep talk. At halftime, the great and much-imitated marching band of Southern performs. Careful observers will note that one of the scoreboards shown at the end of the film is for Lafayette versus Lehigh, one of the game's great rivalries. Even during the pre-game, when the

stands are filling, the filmmakers chose well—the stadium is Michigan's, and the visitor is Penn State. Note the "Joe Pa" sign on the 50-yard line. Whoever made this film—no credits are given—loves college football.

I am sure that the hall has had complaints about the volume of the soundtrack—it is rather loud at points. I am glad that they have so far resisted reducing the volume. If I get to hear Bobby Bowden exhorting his players in the locker room, I want it loud.

Irish fans should be aware that the hall has consciously avoided an overabundance of Notre Dame references throughout, including during this film—Notre Dame is one of many schools shown. Still, you should see this movie twice. Once on the way in, to set the tone for your visit. See it again before you leave to set the mood for the game you will soon see in person. You won't be sorry.

PIGSKIN PAGEANTRY—This section contains some of the museum's sillier exhibits. Do we really need to honor the different ways people tailgate? Do we really need an interactive exhibit where you can try out for a virtual cheerleading squad? This section of the museum, though, does contain one great exhibit—marching bands and fight songs.

At the center of the room is a juke box of sorts, with 24 different college fight songs, along with their sheet music. The songs are all played by the school's own marching band. Hall officials confirm that the "Notre Dame Victory March" is by far the most popular. Notre Dame fans are justifiably proud of their song—*Sports Illustrated* recently called it the greatest of all college fight songs. In the ecumenical spirit of the hall, though, you should listen to a couple of other great fight songs while you're there. Georgia Tech's is a good one, with rousing lyrics about drinking whiskey and being a heck of an engineer. The best, though, other than Notre Dame's, is Tennessee's "Rocky Top." Play the song, close your eyes, and try to imagine 120,000 fans in Volunteer Stadium screaming the words.

THE TRAINING CENTER—This heavily interactive section is the most popular exhibit in the hall. You get to give yourself a complete personal evaluation, and score yourself anywhere from the lowly "Walk

On," to the exalted "Hall of Famer." The training center is divided into three main parts.

• The Fitness Room—Here you get to have the humiliating experience of having your vertical leap, agility, flexibility, and upper body strength measured and scored. There is also a digital scale where, after you weigh yourself, your weight is left displayed, in large, red numbers. I think this whole thing must have been Woody Hayes's idea.

• Practice Field—Pass footballs through small holes, run through a field of tackling dummies, and kick a field goal. Show the scouts that despite your embarrassing showing in the fitness room, you've got what it takes.

• Strategy Clinic—This interesting video quiz is narrated by Mr. College Football, Keith Jackson. Go through four actual strategic scenarios, and then select the play. If you pick the same play as the actual coach did, you get the maximum number of points. The quiz is multiple choice, and is much easier the second or third time through.

THE LOCKER ROOM—The Locker Room is located, appropriately enough, just outside of the training center. In a 12 minute video that is one of the hall's hidden gems, coaches explain the secrets of their craft. The wall on one side of the television monitor is lined with modern lockers, while lockers on the other side represent the leather helmet era. The equipment in all the lockers is interestingly authentic, except for a curious lack of jock straps.

Pantheon: This area lists the recipients of 10 major awards, including the Heisman. Nearby you can also look up the winner of every National Championship, and the winner of every bowl game. Nearby video kiosks show great moments in the game.

• Media: The hall pays tribute to some of the game's great broadcasters. This section also includes the popular "You Call the Play" broadcast booth, where for $5 you can make a tape of yourself calling a play.

• Fields, Footballs, and Officials: Check out the history of footballs, field sizes, and markings. Outstanding college football officials are also honored here.

• Evolution of Equipment: The uniforms of yesterday, plus the evolution of protective equipment. Again, the most protective form of protective equipment is made conspicuous by its absence.

• Rotating Exhibits: The hall frequently changes exhibits to keep things fresh. As was mentioned before, during the season the hall always has an exhibit on that week's Notre Dame opponent. This is usually found in a display case right at the entrance, in front of the reception desk. The hall has also had temporary exhibits on *Sports Illustrated* covers, Woody Hayes, and the evolution of the game program.

After a rocky honeymoon, the future looks bright for the College Football Hall of Fame. It is a beautiful building, and the exhibits are well done. There are enough interactive exhibits to keep even casual fans interested. Executive Director Bernie Kish has weathered the storm

in good enough shape to still be advancing big plans for the hall, like an annual Hall of Fame Game played at Notre Dame Stadium. It looks like the hall is in South Bend for good. There really is no better place for it.

WHILE YOU'RE DOWNTOWN

EAST RACE WATERWAY—St. Joseph River where it crosses LaSalle Street.

One of only six artificial white water courses in the world, and the only one in North America. The US Olympic team trains here, and so can you. Call 219-235-9328 for information.

SOUTH BEND CHOCOLATE COMPANY • 219-233-2577
3300 West Sample Street

Free tour includes short film. Eat a Rockne. Chew on a Domer.

In September 2000, Mark Tarner, company president, announced plans for a Willie Wonka-like tourist attraction and larger chocolate factory downtown along the East Race. The sweet new facility is expected to draw around 30,000 chocoholics in its first year, 2002.

STUDEBAKER NATIONAL MUSEUM • 219-235-9102
525 South Main Street

On the grounds of the legendary factory. Old cars galore, but also includes gems from the company's horse-drawn days, like the carriage that took Lincoln to Ford's Theater.

NORTHERN INDIANA CENTER FOR HISTORY • 219-235-9664
808 West Washington

See the home of a 19th century industrialist, and the home of one of the Polish workers he exploited.

COVELESKI REGIONAL BASEBALL STADIUM • 219-235-9988
501 West South Street, *right next to the Studebaker Museum.*

Everything that is right with minor league baseball. The tickets are cheap, the beer is cold, and the fans are friendly. Home of the South Bend Silver Hawks, an Arizona Diamondbacks' farm club. They are named for a Studebaker car.

Numbers you should know: 10-10

The 1966 Michigan State Game

Ara Parseghian once said that he has been asked about this game every day since it happened—November 19, 1966. It was late in the season, and the undefeated Notre Dame squad was playing Michigan State in East Lansing on national television. Early in the fourth quarter, Coach Parseghian chose to tie the game with a 28-yard field goal, instead of going for a touchdown and the win. His controversial choice resulted in a tie game, the only flaw on the Irish record that season. To understand Ara's choice, you have to understand two conditions that Ara had to contend with that no longer exist.

In 1966, there was no overtime in college football. Games ended in ties regularly. Ara, in fact, coached the Irish in four tie games in his career. The other condition that has changed is that in 1966, Notre Dame didn't play in bowl games. From 1926 until 1969, the university considered bowls incompatible with their academic mission. So, Ara knew that the regular season was his entire season.

Ara also knew that Notre Dame was ranked number one going into the MSU game. He thought that with a tie, he would preserve Notre Dame's position. With a loss, though, Notre Dame would certainly be out of the running. So, he kicked the field goal, and tied the game.

Ara's calculations were correct. Notre Dame won the 1966 National Championship, even with the tie on their record. It would be the first of Ara's two championships. He would win again in

1973, that time going undefeated and untied. Ara retired suddenly in 1974, ending the "era of Ara." His career record at Notre Dame was 95-17-4.

(More recommended reading: **Notre Dame's ERA of ARA** by Tom Pagna with Bob Best published by Diamond Communications, Inc. and available through the Notre Dame bookstore.)

Photo courtesy of the University of Notre Dame Photography Department

Chapter Six

KEEPING THE GAME DAY BODY AND SOUL TOGETHER:
Dining and Drinking

IN 1980, NOTRE DAME FOOD SERVICES pulled Cap'n Crunch cereal out of the dining halls, for reasons that remain obscure. Proving to many that the '60s were indeed dead, the event provoked one of the largest, most coordinated student protests in Notre Dame's history. There were letters to the editor, picket lines, and even sit-ins. In the end, the university relented, and Cap'n Crunch returned triumphantly to the dining halls. Quaker Oats was so touched by the whole thing that they sponsored a three-day Cap'n Crunch festival on campus, which I have to assume is the only Cap'n Crunch Festival ever held anywhere. The Cap'n himself showed up to celebrate. To this day, Cap'n Crunch can always be found in the clear plastic bins in the dining halls. Obviously, the Notre Dame Family has great taste in food.

This chapter will be divided into two parts—on-campus dining and off. Many visitors are surprised at how many dining options they have on campus, and how few they have in town. South Bend lacks the kind of "village" area seen in many college towns—a good bar stool can be hard to find. There are a few important watering holes, though, ones you will want to visit. Game day concession stands on campus and in the stadium will be covered in later chapters.

ON-CAMPUS

DINING HALLS—This is a natural starting point for on-campus dining, since over 75 percent of Notre Dame's students live and eat on campus. You will catch a glimpse of Notre Dame life behind the counter, as well—Notre Dame Food Services employs over 700 students. Two dining halls serve up three meals a day—one hall on the North Quad, and one on the South. Most of the fare reflects the hearty appetites of students—don't look for too many light entrees. In addition, servings are unlimited, including dessert. Now you know the source off the infamous "freshman 15" that many students gain during their first year. Eating in the dining halls will give you a glimpse of students in their natural habitat, so to speak, and visitors are almost always impressed by their unfailing politeness. Don't worry about sticking out as a non-student in a student dining facility—you will be welcome. Around 350 "outsiders" join the students for brunch on game day, and about 450 enjoy the candlelight buffet after the game.

THE SOUTH DINING HALL is the older of the two halls, but is freshly renovated. Built in 1927, it is a prime example of the Gothic Revival, a movement that still affects our impressions of what a college campus should look like. The building's architect, Ralph Adams Cram, was so enamored of the Middle Ages that he advocated the eradication of the internal combustion engine, and a return to walled cities. He successfully modeled the dining hall on the medieval guildhalls.

The South Dining Hall is divided into two giant dining rooms, with the serving area—formerly a public cafeteria known as the Oak Room—between them. Both dining rooms of the South Hall have massive, 35-foot high ceilings, exposed beams, and giant metal chandeliers hanging from dark chains. Both dining rooms have a giant, unused fireplace at one end, and a raised platform at the other. The original purpose of the platform is obvious at first glance—it was where the clerics would take their meals, and keep a close watch on their undergraduate flock. Now

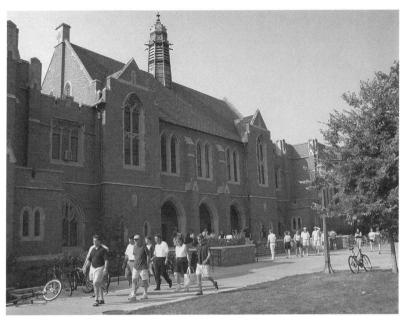

South Dining Hall exterior

South Dining Hall interior

the platform is open to the flock, who prize the seats for the same reason the priests did—it is a prime people-watching vantage point.

The 1997 renovation transformed the South Dining Hall's service area from a standard cafeteria line into a "Food Market." The market area consists of a number of clusters that serve the same type of food every night. There is a Mexican area, for example, and a stir-fry area, a burger area, and a pizza area. Other popular staples include a rotisserie, a salad bar, and a frozen yogurt stand. The entire market area is appointed with a Disneyesque attention to detail. For example: although most bread is baked in Notre Dame's North Quad bakery, the South Dining Hall has a small oven in the market area, just so the aroma of baking bread will be a part of the ambience. With the many options and large serving area, lines are almost non-existent in the South Dining Hall, even in the busiest times.

The renovation was the brainchild of Dave Prentkowski, Notre Dame Food Service's brilliant and dedicated director. He toured the world to study the creative ways in which other people have handled the challenge of serving quality food to large numbers of people. The model he settled on was The Marche, a fabulously successful restaurant in Toronto. Many of Dave's innovations will be invisible to visitors. To-go meals, for example, are now available to busy students, and serving hours are longer. Dave's focus on student quality of life has been welcome and refreshing.

Two works of art within the South Dining Hall deserve a close look. A replica of da Vinci's *Last Supper* hangs in the west dining room. In the food court, two murals adorn the high walls—both were painted in 1942 to celebrate Notre Dame's 100th anniversary. One depicts, among other things, Father Nieuwland's discovery of synthetic rubber. The other depicts various Notre Dame landmarks, including the Log Chapel and the Dome.

THE NORTH DINING HALL serves the other 40-percent-or-so of the students. Students, by the way, are eligible to eat in either hall, so

IN MEMORY OF THE OAK ROOM

For seventy years, the space between the two dining rooms of the South Dining Hall was home to the Oak Room, a public cafeteria. During the Dining Hall's massive 1997 renovation, the Oak Room became the Food Market, and its role as an after-hours source of sustenance was taken over by Recker's, a new Internet café at the back of the hall.

The Oak Room had a majestic, wartime austerity, accentuated by the patriotic murals, the limited menu, and by the warm but barely sufficient incandescent lighting. I ate my first meal at Notre Dame there. I also worked there, and the management did what they could to make the Oak Room "hip." We hosted movie nights, and served nachos. No matter what we did, though, when you walked into the Oak Room, you always felt like you were going back in time. Some of us liked this, and some people didn't. When LaFortune Student Center and The Huddle were remodeled in 1990, the Oak Room suffered.

I became friends with the other Oak Room regulars, a dedicated band who liked the feeling they got when they walked through those huge oak doors on a winter night, looked at the faded murals along the high ceiling, and smelled fresh coffee. In the end, though, the Oak Room didn't have enough advocates. I was glad to hear that the murals had been preserved. I loved that place, though, and I miss it.

that they can go to whichever is most convenient given their hectic schedules. As a rule, though, most students eat in the dining hall closest to their residence hall.

The North Dining Hall was built in 1957, and it originally displayed everything that was wrong with architectural modernism. It was boxy, without ornamentation, and was utterly incongruent with its gothic neighbors, like Farley Hall, next door. As new dorms continued to go up on that side of campus, though, the dining hall needed to expand. The university took the opportunity, in 1987, to add a second story, and revamp the building's prosaic exterior. The results have been great. While not as genuinely gothic or as grandiose as the South Dining Hall, the North Dining Hall is perhaps more comfortable, with carpeting, smaller tables, and a bright, friendly lighting scheme. In the South Dining Hall, you sometimes feel like a vampire might swoop down over you and steal your chicken patty. While this can be exciting, sometimes you just want to eat a sandwich and read the paper.

As for the food: visiting football fans will see Notre Dame Food

Service at its best. Fans wanting to eat a meal in the dining halls can eat brunch before a game, or a candle-lit dinner after the game. The menus at the two halls are almost identical, although the Food Market in the South Dining Hall will offer a little more variety. Brunch is served from 8:00 AM until noon. The standard brunch fare includes eggs, bagels and muffins, fresh fruit, and waffles with a leprechaun on them. The price is $8.25 for adults, and $4.10 for children under 12.

A SEASON OF CANDLELIGHT BUFFETS:
THE MENUS FOR SIX DIFFERENT GAME WEEKENDS

Menu 1• Roast Turkey/Stir Fry Beef/Fried Perch/Lasagna

Menu 2 • Roast Top Sirloin/Chicken Macadamia/Grilled Mahi Mahi/ Spinach Fettuccini

Menu 3 • Roast Top Round/Ginger Fried Chicken/Fresh Gulf Snapper/Cheese Ravioletti

Menu 4 • London Broil/Chicken Tchouptoulas/Poached Salmon/ Fried Cheese Ravioli

Menu 5 • Teriyaki Turkey/Beef Bourguignon/Grilled Trout/ Chinese Noodles

Menu 6 • Bourbon Baked Ham/Chicken Kiev/Lemon Grilled Tuna/ Spinach Tortellini

---

85

After the game, the dining halls put on their best show—the Candle-light Buffet. The service starts at 4:30 and runs until roughly 7:00 PM, although that can change depending on the game. Every week's menu is different, and the dining halls put out a brochure at the beginning of the season which lists the featured items of the buffet. The price for this is $11.50 for adults, and $5.50 for children under 12. As the brochure says, "select anything you want from our menu, and eat as much as you desire in our spacious dining rooms." Dave Prentkowski and Notre Dame Food Services are a credit to Notre Dame. The candlelight buffets are their flagship event.

THE HUDDLE

LaFortune Student Center, built in 1883, was originally Notre Dame's science building. Now the building contains the offices of an array of student organizations, a travel agency, a video rental store, a florist, numerous quiet rooms in which to study, and three restaurants, among other things. The cluster of restaurants within LaFortune is called "The Huddle."

On the main floor of LaFortune are Burger King, and a pizza place called "Tomassito's." Both menus contain few surprises. On the lower floor is Allegro Subs, whose somewhat more eclectic menu includes espresso and genuine Phila-delphia cheesecake.

Back on the main floor is the Huddle Mart. Although not a restaurant, this well-stocked store contains all of the items necessary to satisfy

86

student cravings: mac and cheese, ravioli, and every variety of chips known to man. The Huddle Mart also has a salad bar, soup, candy by the pound, and bagels. Note also the store's non-food items, such as notebooks, toothpaste, and antacids—all things that you might imagine a student needing at some point.

TOP TEN ITEMS SOLD AT THE HUDDLE MART

Studebagels	Coffee
Edy's Ultimate Shake	Minute Made Orange Juice
Bulk Candy	20 oz. Bottle of Coke
Ben & Jerry's Ice Cream	Cup of Soup
Flavored Cappuccino	Deli Sandwiches

RECKER'S

Notre Dame's newest restaurant is named for the school's first student, Clement Recker, who arrived during the winter of 1842. The restaurant was built as part of the expansion of the South Dining Hall that took place in 1997. The menu at Recker's is among the best of the

on-campus eateries—you can choose from pizza cooked in wood-fired ovens, made-to-order burgers, and a variety of deli sandwiches. On one side of Recker's is the "R-Zone," where you can surf the web, send e-mail, or play video games. Another thing that separates Recker's from its on-campus competition are its hours—Recker's is the only on-campus eatery that is open 24 hours a day, seven days a week.

Recker's menu and hours are top notch, but the atmosphere is lacking. There seems to be too much furniture crammed in there, and the overall impression of the place is a little messy. Some of this might be deliberate, given Recker's status as an Internet café, but it doesn't feel hip—just hectic. In addition, the service is slow, and the jumbled tables always seem to be in need of a wiping. The bottom line: if you need a cup of espresso at three in the morning, go ahead and go to Recker's. At any other time, try the Huddle.

SORIN'S (inside the Morris Inn)

Professor Emil T. Hoffman, the legendary teacher of chemistry to thousands of Notre Dame freshman, was also the Dean of Freshmen for decades. During his tenure, he would take every single freshman, two or three at a time, to breakfast at the Morris Inn. It was a nice gesture from a man who could appear stern.

While regular people cannot get a hotel room at the Morris Inn on game weekends, they are welcome in the restaurant. The restaurant became Sorin's in 1999, a steakhouse named for Notre Dame's founder. The interior is a classic assemblage of dark wood and white linen, with fresh flowers on every table. This is not fast food—expect to spend around $10 for breakfast, and $30 for dinner. Besides steak, the dinner menu contains entrees such as Sautéed Foie Gras, Pacific Rim Sea Bass, and Basil Garlic Balsamic Marinated Chicken Breast. A small herb garden just outside the restaurant supplies some of the seasonings. Despite the overall fanciness of the surroundings, Sorin's is flexible about its dress code during game weekends. Of special note to alumni is the bulletin board just inside the Morris Inn's front door. It contains the business cards of on-campus alumni who hope to hook up with old friends.

The place is packed both for breakfast and dinner on game day. You can make reservations at 219-631-2020. The bar, now called "Leahy's," is so small that the Morris Inn has erected a large tent outside the hotel to serve cocktails and food on game days. It, too, is open to the public.

ALUMNI-SENIOR CLUB

One of the great things about being a private university is that you get to have a bar on campus. This one is open only to those students

89

over 21 years of age and alumni. It is located in the stadium's parking lot, in a low slung, non-descript building that some have called the "Alumni Senior Bank" because of its bland exterior. The bar is run by students—the bartender job at "The Club" is one of the most coveted jobs on campus. Since it is run by students, you can be sure that the prices are cheap, and that the emphasis is on fun, with games, music, and drink specials all contributing to that cause. It is not open to the public, but alumni can bring in guests.

THE UNIVERSITY CLUB

Like the Alumni-Senior Club, but without the fun. The club was originally built to be a private facility for Notre Dame faculty, but it now admits members from the community at large, although by invitation only. The club is located across Notre Dame Avenue from and slightly south of the Morris Inn. If you're not a member, you won't get in—don't take it too hard. The High German motif inside consists of a lot of dark leather and giant steins, and is reminiscent of the German restaurant seen in Fast Times at Ridgemont High.

SANDWICH SHOPS

Across the campus, Notre Dame Food Services has a number of smaller restaurants within the larger academic buildings. While these all offer similar menus, each reflects the unique personality of its host building. Waddick's, for example, is located in O'Shaughnessy Hall, the liberal arts building. Waddick's is the place to linger over coffee and debate Jung. Common Stock, located in the basement of the Business School, serves up fresh *Wall Street Journal*s with its coffee. The official hours for all of these smaller sandwich shops have them close on weekends, but some of them have special Saturday hours during the football season.

Sandwich Shop	Open on Game Day	Location
Waddick's	Yes	O'Shaughnessy Hall South Quad
Common Stock	No	College of Business Administration Debartolo Quad
Café Poche	Yes	Bond Hall (Architecture Building) South Quad
Greenfields Café	No	Hesburgh Center for International Studies Debartolo Quad
Irish Café	Yes	Law School South Quad
Café De Grasta	No	Grace Hall Mod Quad

THE PIT IN THE LIBRARY

The basement of the library contains the one dining area on campus untouched by the recent wave of renovation—it is a perfectly preserved relic of the Formica age. One wall is lined with phone booths, and the other with vending machines of the rotating-carousel-of-food variety. The most popular vending machine sandwich? PB&J, of course. The tiled anteroom that leads to the Pit contains three white telephones and nothing else—not even a chair for the phone users. It looks like cross between a Dali painting and the room in a prison where inmates get to call their lawyers. During the academic year, the low-ceilinged

Pit is loud with the voices of students, who are eager to talk and eat a bag of cheetos after hours of quiet studying in the spaces above. For an authentic Notre Dame experience, descend into the Pit, and choke down a PB&J.

OFF-CAMPUS

As was mentioned earlier, South Bend lacks the kind of "village" area typical of most college towns. The bars and restaurants that are student hangouts are spread across South Bend, making it hard for visiting fans to locate the prime watering holes. As in any town, there are many restaurants that are continuously changing names, owners, and motifs. There are also representatives of all the chains that you would expect to find in a medium-sized city: the Outback, Chili's, the Olive Garden, etc. The restaurants and taverns mentioned here, though, have withstood the test of time, are unique to the area, and hold some special significance for the Notre Dame family.

CORBY'S
441 E. LaSalle Street
South Bend
219-233-5326

Parts of *Rudy* were filmed here, as you will read in every single one of Corby's ads. You remember the scene—Rudy is chillin', having a few brews, with genuine Celtic music playing in the background. After one too many, he spills the beans to his true love—he's not really a Notre Dame student! So she has to kick him off the booster squad! Stupid Rudy! Anyhow, that happened at Corby's. Funny thing, though—this wasn't the real Corby's.

The real Corby's was part of the legendary five-corners bar district of Edison Street. All the bars there are closed now, due to a deteriorating neighborhood, and to repeated violations of state law regarding the minimum drinking age. Only Bridget McGuire's lives on—as a coffee house. Corby's lives on in its new location, as a matter of fact, because of *Rudy*. Because the real Corby's was just a memory, Hollywood commandeered the downtown bar, known at the time as the Cap n' Cork, to film the bar scenes. When filming ended, the owners decided to keep the name, and capitalize on their new fame.

So, the real Rudy probably never said anything stupid to a woman in this Corby's. Unless, of course, he has said it in the last seven years. Be a part of that tradition.

THE LINEBACKER
1631 South Bend Avenue
South Bend
219-289-0186

The closest of the important bars, the Linebacker stands just across Edison from the Jamison Inn. The bar contains a predictable amount of ND paraphernalia, along with a happening seventies record collection that they probably acquired during the '70s. The bar is dark, loud, and somewhat grimy on the inside, just like you remember it. One nice thing about the Linebacker is that it has always been one of the few bars where Notre Dame students and South Bend residents manage to coexist peacefully.

CJ's
417 N. Michigan Street
South Bend
219-233-5981

If you want to go to a bar where you might actually see Notre Dame football players, this is the place. That cachet is really the only thing that distinguishes CJs— it is a somewhat dark downtown bar with a pool table and a smelly bathroom. Many Notre Dame students, though, eager for life experiences that might shock their parents, have made CJ's their bar of choice. And, as I said, it is known as the players' bar. If you should see a football player in there, though, the night before the game, please tell him to immediately return to his room.

COACH'S
2046 South Bend Ave.
South Bend
219-277-7678

This, the newest of the four important bars, is only slightly farther from campus than the Linebacker. It is a prototypical sports bar, with giant projection televisions, dartboards, and a basketball goal. They also have a better than average menu for a bar, which includes the Personal Fowl, a barbecue chicken sandwich. Very popular with students, Coach's is crowded on weekends throughout the year. Coach's has a unique promotional item—a business-card sized piece of paper, with a triangular cutout made such that you can stick it onto the rim of your glass. It says "GONE TO PEE—LEAVE MY DRINK ALONE." Ask for one.

MACRI'S
227 University
South Bend
219-277-7273

Macri's is now a small chain, with franchises in the other college towns of Indiana—Bloomington and West Lafayette. It started in South Bend, though, and the place still has a devoted following. The décor is pure sports bar, including a shelf with hats representing Notre Dame's opponents. A basketball scoreboard dominates the main dining room, and indicates that Notre Dame is playing UCLA—a great conversation starter for ND basketball loyalists.

Macri's specializes in hot subs on fresh bread—their biggest seller is the BRT—bacon, roast beef and tomato. They also have a number of popular croissant sandwiches for those looking for a lighter meal. Also popular is their "Big Beer," a thirty-two ounce monstrosity.

TIPPECANOE PLACE
620 West Washington St.
South Bend
219-234-9077

If Macri's is home of the Big Beer, then Tippecanoe Place is the home of the Big Check. This is, without question, South Bend's nicest restaurant, and it is where generations of Notre Dame parents have taken their sons and daughters to dinner when in town.

The restaurant is located in the former home of Clement Studebaker.

Studebaker had made a fortune during the Civil War by selling wagons to the Union Army. He built the mansion in 1889. It is a spectacular example of Richardsonian Romanesque architecture, and is a window on an era when the very rich were expected to display their wealth in a very public way. The house has 40 rooms, 20 fireplaces, and a grand staircase that has been photographed in countless wedding parties.

While Tippecanoe's is fancy, its prices are actually a pleasant surprise—its dinners are in the $15-$20 range. The Sunday brunch is a downright bargain: $11.95 for adults, $7.95 for children 5-12, and free for the tykes under 5. Make reservations, and allow yourself time to wander through the house.

THE OUTBACK
4611 Grape Road
Mishawaka
219-271-2333

Although it's not unique to Michiana, this area Outback makes the book at the insistence of my publisher. The wait for a table can be lengthy at times, but she says it's worth it (even if you do have to manuever the madness of Grape Road) because the service is friendly, the servings tasty, and the suds cold. It's a favorite of many ND students, too, including some football players looking for a hearty snack.

BRUNO'S
2610 Prairie Avenue
South Bend
219-288-3320

Head a bit southwest of campus for some of the finest and (most

filling!) pizza you'll ever have the pleasure to devour. Bruno's is legendary in the area for its hearty "pie" (including a "white" pizza that has no sauce but instead is topped with veggies, shrimp, and feta cheese), great selection of pasta and sauces, and sandwiches. Bruno's offers carry-out too and a full bar (the bar stays).

THE VINE
122 South Michigan
South Bend
219-234-9463

As suggested by the name, The Vine is a small but classy restaurant featuring a wide assortment of fine wines to accompany pasta, salads, and gourmet pizza. The prices are very reasonable, and the appetizers alone make this restaurant worth a visit. Located downtown, in the same block as The College Football Hall of Fame and The South Bend Chocolate Company Cafe, The Vine is also within walking distance of several area clubs.

THE SOUTH BEND
CHOCOLATE COMPANY CAFÉ
122 South Michigan
Phone: 219-287-0725

If you're in the mood for something sweet while you're in town, pay a visit to the The Chocolate Cafe, located downtown next to The

College Football Hall of Fame and The Vine restaurant. In addition to their signature-line of locally-made chocolates, the cafe offers a variety of coffees, ice cream, and cheesecakes smooth enough to satisfy any sweet tooth. Before you go, be sure to pick up a box of Rocknes or Domers for those unfortunate souls who couldn't make the trip.

ROCCO'S
537 N. St. Louis Boulevard
South Bend
219-233-2464

Home of "South Bend's Original Pizza," Rocco's sits on the corner of South Bend Avenue and St. Louis on one of the only hillsides in South Bend. The building is somewhat odd-looking, and inside the décor is simple, but if it's looks you're going for—head to Tippecanoe Place. If it's great traditional food you want, then don't pass up the Rocco's experience—"A Student Tradition Since 1951." The pizza is delicious (though a bit a pricey) and the menu offers a wide variety of authentic Italian cuisine, cooked up with a whole lot of family tradition, too.

K'S GRILL & PUB
1733 South Bend Avenue
Phone: 219-277-2527

Located one mile east of campus, K's is a great spot for relaxing

with friends over a beer or a root beer float. They have everything from Chicago dogs and 1/3 lb. burgers with the works to veggie pitas, homemade soups and shakes, and specialty sandwiches like Knute's Delight and The Heisman. The prices are decent, the food is good, and the kids' menu allows those traveling with tykes to take a welcome break from the golden arches.

You'll find numerous other sources of sustenance and spirits within reasonable distance of campus. Here's a brief listing of some of them:

PARISI'S
1412 South Bend Avenue
South Bend
219-232-4244

NICOLA'S
1705 South Bend Avenue
South Bend
219-277-5666

LA ESPERANZA
1636 North Ironwood Drive
South Bend
219-273-0345

MANDARIN HOUSE
2304 Edison Road
South Bend
219-287-4414

NICK'S PATIO
1710 N. Ironwood Drive
South Bend
219-277-7400

BW-3
123 W. Washington
South Bend
219-232-2293

THE EMPORIUM
121 South Niles
South Bend
219-234-9000

STUDEBAGELS
1801 South Bend Avenue
South Bend
219-277-4440

Numbers you should know: 11

Notre Dame's National Championships

The College Football National Championship is sometimes referred to as a "mythical" title, because it has been customarily determined by a poll rather than in a playoff system, or in a championship game. Since the game began, a number of polls and formulas have fallen in and out of favor—the Bowl Championship Series is the latest incarnation. Notre Dame has won 11 consensus National Championships—more than any other school.

YEAR	RECORD	COACH
1924	10-0	Knute Rockne
1929	9-0	Knute Rockne
1930	10-0	Knute Rockne
1943	9-1	Frank Leahy
1946	8-0-1	Frank Leahy
1947	9-0	Frank Leahy
1949	10-0	Frank Leahy
1966	9-0-1	Ara Parseghian
1973	11-0	Ara Parseghian
1977	11-1	Dan Devine
1988	12-0	Lou Holtz

Lou Holtz coached the Irish to their most recent National Championship in 1988.
Photograph courtesy of the University of Notre Dame Photography Department.

Chapter Seven

NUMBER ONE MOSES AND TOUCHDOWN JESUS:
A Walking Tour

NOTRE DAME DOES not allow new students to have cars. Only after they have completed their first semester, demonstrated a certain academic rigor, and obtained permission from the dean may they drive at Notre Dame. Don't pity the freshmen—cars have never been an integral part of life at Notre Dame. Even those students who have cars mostly live on campus, and walk from class to class to residence hall to dining hall. Notre Dame has no thru-streets, no gas stations, no parking meters, and no parking garages. Every change to the campus is made with the pedestrian student in mind. To walk the entire long, east-west axis of the campus, walk from the old ROTC building, now home to campus security, to the new ROTC building. You can complete this trip in just 15 minutes. I know, because during my last summer at Notre Dame I made this walk about two thousand times, helping my Navy ROTC unit make the move.

This chapter will take you on a much more leisurely walking tour of the campus, one that you could take anytime, not just on a game weekend. Along the way, we'll see the notable landmarks that should be a part of anyone's trip to Notre Dame. Those campus sights and sounds unique to a football weekend will be covered in the next chapter.

Before we start walking, here is a broad overview to help acquaint you with the fundamentals of Notre Dame's geography.

NOTRE DAME GEOGRAPHY 101

QUADS: The buildings of Notre Dame are, for the most part, arranged along the sides of five main quadrangles or "quads." These are: North Quad, South Quad, Main Quad, Mod Quad, and the new one, the DeBartolo Quad. North, South, and the Main Quads make up the older heart of the campus.

LAKES: Notre Dame's northwestern corner is defined by two large, natural lakes: St. Mary's Lake and St. Joseph's Lake. St. Mary's Road runs on the land bridge between the two lakes, and has seen the brisk, hopeful footsteps of generations of Notre Dame men.

ROADS: As was mentioned earlier, Notre Dame is intentionally unaccommodating to the automobile. The main roads that approach Notre Dame run around and not into the campus. In very rough terms, four roads make a box around the campus. **Douglas Road** makes up the northern boundary. **Angela**, which becomes **Edison**, is the southern boundary. **Highway 31** makes up the western boundary, and also separates Notre Dame from St. Mary's. **Juniper Road** is the rough eastern boundary of the campus, and is the road that runs between Notre Dame Stadium and the Joyce ACC.

Notre Dame Avenue runs north-south, and points directly at the Golden Dome of the Main Building. It ends before then, though, at the Main Circle, with the statue *Our Lady of the University*. Notre Dame Avenue doesn't really go anywhere, but it makes up for this lack of substance with style. The road provides a dramatic approach to the Main Quad, especially in the fall, when the large hardwoods that line it are bursting with color. If you are visiting Notre Dame on any day other that the actual day of a football game, you will find that the parking lot of the Eck Center, accessible from Notre Dame Avenue, is one of the largest and most convenient parking lots available to visitors. The Eck Center is the best place to start our walking tour.

Eck Notre Dame Visitors' Center exterior

Eck Notre Dame Visitors' Center interior

ECK NOTRE DAME VISITORS' CENTER

The Eck Center is a two-building complex that houses three important facilities. The smaller building houses the Visitors' Center and the Alumni Association office. The larger building is the Hammes Bookstore. Notre Dame is the second most popular tourist destination in Indiana, second only to the Indianapolis Motor Speedway. Incredibly, until 1999, these legions of visitors had no central gathering place at Notre Dame. That's when Frank Eck, class of 1944, donated $10 million to the university for this project.

Inside Mr. Eck's building, visitors walk into a bright, airy, welcoming space. Glass cases house small exhibits along the wall, such as photos of the library under construction. Mainly, though, there is a feeling of openness, a pleasing sensation for those about to endure the claustrophobic crowds of a football weekend. Extraordinarily friendly people give away maps, mass schedules, and recommendations at the information desk at the center of the center. If they can't answer your questions, they will know who can. The center periodically publishes a small pamphlet: "Suggested Sites to Visit on the University of Notre Dame Campus." If you want the luxury of a tour guide, the center offers free tours conducted by ND students. The tours start at 11:00 AM and 3:00 PM, Monday through Friday. The guided tour takes between 90 minutes and two hours.

One of the best ways to start your visit is in the Eck Center's 152-seat auditorium. You may have to request the staff to start it, but watch the 12-minute film there that describes Notre Dame's history and culture. It is exceptionally well done. Especially inspiring are the excerpts from Ronald Reagan's speech at Notre Dame, when he says, "let them come, to Notre Dame." Listen to the man.

THE HAMMES BOOKSTORE

The old bookstore is a smoldering hole in the ground now, just about in the middle of the South Quad. You may be tempted to think

that the small size of that hole is an optical illusion, but it is not—the old bookstore was really that small. Not only did every student's textbook come out of that tiny building, but so did most of the sweatshirts, hats, and leprechaun shot glasses that flowed into the hands of alumni during game weekends. In those days, you actually had to wait in line to even get inside the bookstore, like some sort of bizarre blue and gold Studio 54. A highly placed campus official told me that back then, when the university was recruiting a professor, they would actually avoid the bookstore—it was seen as kind of an embarrassment. Now, though, thanks to the generosity of Mr. Eck, I suspect that the bookstore is one of the first things they see.

The downstairs of the bookstore is devoted, in large part, to Notre Dame logo merchandise, such as hats, shirts, steins, and key chains. One of the more notable sections is the desk where class rings are ordered—students can't order their ring until their Junior year. There is also a large section of religious items, such as Rosary beads and Catechisms. The downstairs also contains a coffee bar and a grand piano.

The upstairs area is devoted mostly to textbooks, although a few souvenirs can be found. The cashier upstairs is no longer a secret on game days—expect equally lengthy lines throughout the store.

After exceeding your souvenir budget, head west to the building that "caps" the western end of the South Quad—the Rockne Memorial Gym.

Hammes Bookstore

ROCKNE MEMORIAL GYM

The "Rock" was built in 1938 as a memorial to the great coach, who died in 1931. Its facilities are open to students and faculty only, and the famously athletic student body makes good use of them. The gym contains an Olympic-size swimming pool, weight rooms, racquetball courts, and more. Newer, shinier athletic facilities have been built on campus, like Rolfs Aquatic Center and the Eck Tennis Pavilion. At the Rockne, though, with its insufficient incandescent lighting, legendary namesake, and sporting figures carved into stone, you just can't help but think that you are getting a better workout.

Even though the athletic facilities are not open to the general public, the lobby of the Rock is accessible. There is a little-seen collection of Rockne memorabilia there, and a bronze statue of Knute himself, whose nose has been rubbed shiny by generations of students.

LYONS ARCH

After leaving through the front door of the Rock, turn left, and head for the residence hall that makes up that corner of the quad. Its arch is a "must see" on our walking tour.

The arch in Lyons Hall looks towards St. Mary's lake, and is one of the nicer architectural features on the campus. The rooms east of the arch and over the arch were originally designed to be the home of faculty, so as you might expect they are a cut above the normal undergraduate housing. Today, the rooms are highly prized by Lyons Seniors. Lyons, by the way, is a women's dorm, and has been so since 1974.

Right next to Lyons is Morrissey Hall, a men's hall. Facing Lyons is Howard Hall, another women's hall, and home to another notable arch.

HOWARD ARCHES

These two, parallel arches, in addition to being a pleasant architectural feature, allow passage from one end of the South Quad to another. Howard, like Lyons, is a women's dormitory. Howard wasn't

converted until 1987, though,
and the change caused much
controversy on campus. Men
who had lived and bonded in
Howard for their entire collegiate careers were scattered
across campus. They protest-
ed by hanging banners from
the windows of Howard saying, "Walk like an Eviction."
Residents of Badin, the
women's dorm next door,
hung bedsheet signs out their
windows saying, "No Chicks

Next Door." Back then, though, men still outnumbered women on campus by about three-to-one, and the university was determined to make
their numbers equal. Female housing was one of the main limitations,
so something had to give. Today, young men and women are present in
roughly equal numbers on Notre Dame's campus.

Keep walking straight after you pass through the arch, until you
find yourself in the middle of the Main Quad. Walk to the Golden Dome,
officially known as the Main Building.

MAIN BUILDING

The Golden Dome of the main building is the most recognizable
landmark on campus, with the possible exception of Touchdown Jesus.
While the building's mission has been defined and redefined continuously over the years, it has always held some combination of class-
rooms and administrative offices. The Main Building was built in 1879,
after fire destroyed a sizable portion of the fledgling university's buildings. The new building was considered lavish and excessive even by
some of Notre Dame's own during its construction. Father Sorin, though,

Notre Dame's redoubtable founder, insisted on a grand monument to the possibilities of his school. In fact, he took the fire of 1879 as a sign from God that he had not been thinking big enough. No one could accuse him of that after the building was completed.

The Golden Dome itself is the focal point of the entire campus, both physically and psychologically. Notre Dame students and alumni call themselves "Domers" in honor of the building. People who go on to get their master's degree from ND are called "double domers" which also used to be the name of a hamburger sold at The Huddle before Burger King took over. The helmets of the football players are gold in honor of the dome.

The gold leaf that covers the dome is three microns thick—three millionths of a meter. Only eight ounces of 23-carat gold hammered this thin was enough to cover the entire dome during its latest re-gilding, in 1988. The statue of Mary on top is 19 feet tall and weighs 4,400 pounds. The top of that statue is 225 feet above the ground.

The Main Building was closed for two years, from July 1997 to July

1999, for a massive renovation. The renovation cost $58 million—it cost only $1 million to build the Dome in 1879. Even if you've been in the Main Building a dozen times, you must return to see it since this rebirth.

BASILICA OF THE SACRED HEART

Right next door to the Dome is the Sacred Heart Basilica. This church took over 20 years to build—from 1870 to 1892. The cross that tops Sacred Heart is the highest structure on campus at 230 feet—five feet higher than the statue of Mary on the dome.

The church was designated a basilica in 1992 by Pope John Paul II, and is one of only 40 churches in the United States to achieve this status. Like the Main Building, Sacred Heart benefited from a recent multi-million dollar renovation. Sacred Heart got its facelift from 1988 to 1990, at a total cost of $7.5 million. One of the main efforts during this renovation was to restore the church's many stained glass windows, which were originally constructed the Carmelite nuns of Le Mans, France, in the 19th century.

Another similarity to the Main Building is the presence of artwork by Luis Gregori—the artist who was recruited away from the Vatican by the persuasive Father Sorin. His most famous works at Notre Dame are the murals that depict the life of Columbus in the Main Building. He also painted the Stations of the Cross and the Life of Mary in Sacred Heart.

The east entrance to the basilica is famous for the slogan "God, Country, Notre Dame," carved in stone above the doorway. The door is a memorial to Notre Dame veterans.

Sacred Heart contains a small museum of its own, which contains vintage vestments and other artifacts of the Catholic Church. Sacred Heart has so much to see that it has its own cadre of dedicated volunteer guides, whose ranks include my father-in-law. Call them at 219-631-7329 for tour information.

THE GROTTO

Nestled between the Basilica and the lakes is Notre Dame's other famous religious landmark—The Grotto.

The full name is The Grotto of Our Lady of Lourdes. It was built in 1896 as a one-seventh-scale representation of the famous shrine at Lourdes, France. While Sacred Heart is the preferred location for Notre Dame weddings, the grotto has long been the preferred location for Notre Dame marriage proposals. This is fitting—Sacred Heart is the

grand cathedral for public ceremony, while the Grotto is a place of private reflection.

Candles are lit by the prayerful at the Grotto at all hours, and many regular visitors make the Grotto their first stop on campus. In 1985, before the Michigan game, so many candles were lit that the Grotto actually caught fire.

LAKES

If you want to lengthen your tour, the Grotto is a perfect launching pad for a stroll around either one of Notre Dame's lakes. Looking out from the Grotto, St. Mary's Lake is to your left, and St. Joseph's Lake is to the right. Both lakes have well-defined, well-travelled paths that surround them. Both lakes reward the walker with some nice views of campus, and some little known sights.

SIGHTS AROUND ST. MARY'S LAKE

• The Security Building—formerly the ROTC building, which was formerly one of a dozen buildings built in 1943 by the United States Navy to house their massive training facility on Notre Dame's campus.

This pink building was left standing, and was home to all three of Notre Dame's ROTC units until 1990, when I personally helped move the entire building's contents to the new Pasquerilla Center, one box at a time.

- Carroll Hall—One of Notre Dame's loneliest residence halls. Famous for its Halloween Haunted House, and its team nickname. Residents of Carroll call themselves "The Vermin."
- Fatima Retreat House and Shrine
- The ghost of Holy Cross Hall—On the northern shore of St. Mary's lake, a road leads up a slight rise—to nowhere. The attentive will find a small plaque that notes the former location of one of Notre Dame's most storied residence halls: Holy Cross. Holy Cross residents

were famous for their camaraderie, their hard drinking, and for their dangerous walk across the lake as soon as it was frozen, but before it was really safe. The hall was closed in 1990, and was demolished soon after. I walked the entire cleared area there, thinking I could find some low brick wall, a hearthstone, or maybe even a hollow area marking the location of the building's foundation. I couldn't find anything. Other than the plaque, and the memories of a thousand Notre Dame men, nothing is left of Holy Cross Hall.

SIGHTS AROUND ST. JOSEPH'S LAKE

- Columba Hall—a brothers' residence
- St. Joseph Hall—The Scared Heart Parish Center
- Moreau Seminary—This seminary is also the sight of Notre Dame President Monk Malloy's twice-weekly pick-up basketball games.

- The Beach and Boathouse—The boathouse serves both Notre Dame's rowing team, and the Navy ROTC unit, which requires a basic sailing qualification of its midshipmen. The beach sees crowds of students during that small sliver of the school year when it is warm enough to swim in a spring-fed northern Indiana lake.

STEPAN CENTER

Due east of the boathouse is the distinctive, if not picturesque, Stepan Center. This multi-purpose geodesic dome, built in 1962, is one of the best preserved examples of George Jetson architecture in the United States. Stepan used to be important to football fans in its role as the home of the Friday night pep rally. The building's bad acoustics, remote location, and small interior have since moved the rallies to other locations.

Stepan Center caps the northern end of what is affectionately known as the Mod Quad. The name effectively denotes the fact that the buildings are not just modern, but actually possess that certain kind of modernity that looks especially dated. The two 11-story towers that are the Mod Quad's most noticeable feature are Grace and Flanner. Both were built in 1969 as residence halls, but both were converted recently into office space.

Near Stepan Center and the rest of the Mod Quad is a little known landmark of special interest to football fans—the fire station. During the legendary football seasons of the 1940s, Coach Frank Leahy would actually live in an upstairs bedroom of the fire station—#7 West.

WARREN GOLF COURSE

Located northeast of campus on the corner of Angela and Douglas Roads is the beautiful new 18-hole Warren Golf Course. Designed by professional golfer Ben Crenshaw, the course is carved out of 250 wooded acres and, from the back tees, spans 6,744 yards. You'll find lots of water, sand, and trees—but no par for the course! That's right, perhaps

the most unique feature of the Warren is the fact that only yardage is measured for each hole, allowing players to pick their own par. Dedicated in May of 2000, the Warren includes a 7,000-foot clubhouse, (where you'll find the Warren Grille and pro shop), a driving range, and putting green. For more information about greens fees and tee times during home football game weekends, call the Warren Golf Course at (219) 631-4653.

Note: The original Notre Dame Golf Course, which lost nine holes due to construction of new dorms, remains open as does its pro shop in the Rockne Memorial. For more information about game day scheduling, call (219) 631-6425.

CLARKE MEMORIAL FOUNTAIN

The fountain that caps the south end of the North Quad goes by many names. It was originally christened in 1986 as the War Memorial, which caused some noisy protests by ND's small but dedicated band of

peaceniks. It is now officially called the Clarke Memorial Fountain, after a university benefactor Maude Clarke. Most often, the fountain is called Stonehenge.

The fountain is a monument to the Notre Dame alumni who made the ultimate sacrifice in World War II, Korea, and Viet Nam. The Latin inscription on the fountain is Pro Patria et Pace—For Country and Peace. Notre Dame is one of the country's most patriotic college campuses. The university is home to ROTC units for each of the three military services, and each has been cited in recent years as the best unit in the country. Almost 10 percent of Notre Dame's students attend school on a ROTC scholarship. In the three wars that the fountain memorializes, over 500 Notre Dame men gave their lives. Despite the protests, this is something that deserves to be honored.

Photo credit: Susie & Todd Tucker

The War Memorial sits in the middle of Fieldhouse Mall. The Fieldhouse was the famously noisy home of Notre Dame's basketball team until it was replaced by the ACC in 1968. The building was demolished in 1983, but the "April 1898" cornerstone has been turned into a small, easily missed monument just west of the War Memorial.

THEODORE M. HESBURGH LIBRARY

Look east from Stonehenge, and you will have an uninterrupted line of sight to the most recognizable collegiate library in the world—our next stop.

It is hard to determine Father Hesburgh's greatest contribution to the university during his 35-year tenure as president. Hesburgh himself has said that gaining the admission of women to the school in 1972 was his greatest accomplishment. Certainly, Hesburgh's most lasting physical monument at the school will be the massive library. For that reason, the name of the library was changed from Memorial Library to honor him upon his retirement in 1987.

The building was opened in 1963, and was the largest collegiate library in the world at that time. Someone once calculated that the

Photo credit: Susie & Todd Tucker

14-story building could comfortably accommodate half of the entire student body at one time. It actually does accommodate an impressive 2.5 million volumes. It is the center of serious study at Notre Dame, although the degree of seriousness tends to vary directly with altitude. In general, the higher you go in the library, the more serious the scholarship. In the noisy basement snack bar, no scholarship takes place. On the wide-open second floor, studying and socializing occur in roughly equal proportions. As you ascend to the higher floors, quiet reading predominates. The higher floors are a great place to get an elevated view of the campus, but be considerate of the scholars.

Two major works of art associated with the library have acquired football nicknames. Most famous is "Touchdown Jesus," actually entitled *The Word of Life*. The giant mosaic depicts Christ as The Teacher. Almost immediately upon its completion, people noticed that Christ's outstretched arms seemed to be signaling a touchdown. The connection was natural enough, since the mural is clearly visible from inside the stadium. The library's other work of art with a football nickname is statue of Moses pointing skyward just outside the library. The artist was

depicting Moses's assertion that there is only one true God. Notre Dame students thought that Moses might also be asserting Notre Dame's position in the polls.

JOYCE ATHLETIC AND CONVOCATION CENTER (JACC)

Exit the library on the side opposite from where we came in. This side of the library fronts Juniper Road. Just a short walk

south takes us to the center of spectator sports at the university. On the west side of Juniper is Notre Dame Stadium, a structure we will discuss in detail in Chapter Nine. Across the street from the stadium are the distinctive twin domes of the Joyce Athletic and Convocation Center.

The Joyce Athletic and Convocation Center is where Notre Dame plays basketball, a cute sport that helps pass the time between football seasons. It was built in 1968, and was originally named the Athletic and Convocation Center. It was renamed in 1987, in honor of Father Ned Joyce's retirement. He served the school for many years as Father Hesburgh's executive vice president.

The JACC consists of two domes. The south dome is home to the school's main basketball arena. The northern dome is home to Notre Dame's ice hockey team, and a multipurpose area that sees much traffic on game days—we'll get into that more in the next chapter. On the second floor concourse between the two domes is a place worth seeking out—The Sports Heritage Hall.

The names of every single person to ever win a varsity letter in any sport at Notre Dame are arranged along the ceiling, in a chronological listing. In the display cases that line the walls is Notre Dame's largest public display of sports memorabilia. Heisman trophies, bowl trophies, and vintage photographs make this place a Mecca for Notre Dame junkies. Look carefully—there are some real gems in here. Try to find the letter Bear Bryant wrote to the university upon his retirement, where he declares for the record that he never beat Notre Dame. Alabama fans hate that.

The JACC sits across Juniper from the football stadium. On the other side of the stadium is Notre Dame's newest quad, and our last stop: the DeBartolo Quad.

DEBARTOLO QUAD

The name is familiar to even those football fans who don't follow Notre Dame. Ed DeBartolo, Jr., was the owner and president of the San Francisco Forty-niners during their ascendancy in the National Football League. Their field general at that time, you may remember, was another Notre Dame graduate, Joe Montana, class of 1979. Ed DeBartolo, Sr., class of 1932, donated $33 million to Notre Dame in 1989 to build this quad. It remains the largest individual gift in Notre Dame history.

His money helped fund the construction of the three main buildings that make up this quad. DeBartolo Hall is a huge multi-purpose

building that covers over four acres. Next door is the College of Business Administration. Across the quad is the Hesburgh Center for International Studies.

This new quad, despite its location adjacent to the stadium, is one of the least visited areas on campus by fans. This is especially interesting because the area used to be hallowed ground for football fans, in its prior life as "Green Field." Green Field was the best place to tailgate, bar none, a tradition that ended promptly upon construction of the quad. The wide open spaces that comprise the quad may alone make it worth a visit during a hectic game weekend—note especially the peaceful Sesquicentennial Common at the north end of the quad.

The Sesquicentennial Commons was built in 1992 to celebrate the university's 150th anniversary. It consists of a fountain and a series of white, airy arches, and comfortable benches. The light style is a pleasant contrast to the university's normal gothic brick-and-gargoyle motif. Stop here a while and rest. Our walking tour is over, but our work has just begun.

Numbers you should know: 7

Notre Dame's Seven Heisman Trophy Winners

The John W. Heisman Memorial Trophy, awarded by the Downtown Athletic Club of New York, is the most prestigious individual award in college football. Seven Notre Dame players have won the trophy, more than from any other school.

1. 1943—Angelo Bertelli

Bertelli came to Notre Dame from Springfield, Massachusetts, where the quarterback was known as "The Springfield Rifle." In 1943, his senior year at Notre Dame, Bertelli played just six games before leaving school to join the Marine Corps, and the war. Despite the abbreviated season, Bertelli was the runaway winner of the Heisman.

2. 1947—John Lujack

Lujack played quarterback, defensive back, and punted during his career at Notre Dame. He also won back-to-back National Championships in 1946 and 1947. He had a successful professional career, playing four seasons with the Chicago Bears.

3. 1949—Leon Hart

Leon Hart is the only lineman to ever win the Heisman Trophy. He never lost a game during his career at Notre Dame, going 36-0-2 under Coach Leahy. As a pro with the Detroit Lions, Hart was named an all-pro player on both offense and defense in 1951.

4. 1953—John Lattner

Lattner was another of Notre Dame's multi-talented Heisman winners. He played in halfback, defensive back, and punter. He

Tim Brown, 1987 Heisman Trophy Winner, University of Notre Dame.
Photograph courtesy of the University of Notre Dame Photography Deparment.

won the Heisman in one of the closest votes in history, beating Paul Giel of Minnesota by a vote of 1,850 to 1,794.

5. 1956—Paul Hornung

Paul Hornung is the only player from a team with a losing record to win the Heisman—the Irish were 2-8 in 1956. While primarily known as a quarterback, the "Golden Boy" was also an effective defensive back—he intercepted five passes during his junior year.

6. 1964—John Huarte

Quarterback John Huarte was the cornerstone of Ara Parseghian's rebuilding at Notre Dame. His senior year, 1964, was Ara's first at Notre Dame. Huarte threw for 2,062 yards in that season.

7. 1987—Tim Brown

Before his senior year even began, *Sports Illustrated* called him "the best player on the land." Brown was an explosive flanker, but his most memorable moments came as a kick returner. In the 1987 game against Michigan State, he returned two punts for touchdowns—in a row.

Chapter Eight

WARM BEER AT SUNRISE:
Pre-game

MOST SCHOOLS GO OUT of their way to foster tailgating, hosting hospitality tents, radio station promotions, contests, and other such wackiness. Not Notre Dame. The administration has long viewed tailgating as a sort of necessary evil, and has gone out of its way in recent years to limit the parking lot partying. For example, as was already mentioned, recreational vehicles are no longer allowed to park overnight on university property. The construction of the DeBartolo quad eliminated some of ND's best tailgating areas. Students caught hosting tailgaters—with alcohol—suffer $300 fines. The event "tailgating" is not listed on any university schedule, and its location is not listed on any map.

Great tailgating still exists—you just have to know where to look. We'll get to that. The thing you need to keep in mind, though, is that pre-game at Notre Dame is much more than tailgating. It is a festival, full of more activities and rituals than you could ever hope to see in those few hours between sunrise and kick-off. Notre Dame can downplay tailgating only because it has this wealth of activities to offer visiting fans.

Many of these activities take place at different times on different football weekends, due to the vagaries of network television schedules.

The best document to help you keep track of your specific weekend's itinerary is the "Things to do on Campus" flyer published by the Alumni Association. It is a single-page document, printed on both sides and folded in half. This data-rich publication is filled with the times and locations for every university-endorsed pre-game activity that occurs between Friday and Sunday. You can pick the flyer up at locations all over campus, like the Huddle, the South Dining Hall, or in the lobby of the Morris Inn. Out in town, some hotels even stock the flyer for their game-bound guests.

Another good publication to look for upon your arrival is the Friday edition of *The Observer*, Notre Dame's daily student newspaper. In addition to a complete schedule of weekend events, the *Observer's* outstanding sports section will help you study up for the game. *The Observer* is free, and stacks of them can be found across campus.

A Typical Pre-game Weekend
THURSDAY
6:00 PM DILLON PEP RALLY (first home game only)

For years, Dillon Hall, a men's residence hall, has hosted its own, intense pep rally on the Thursday evening before the first home game. The rally had an improvised flavor for many years, but it has become more organized and sophisticated with each passing year. Lou Holtz, for example, became an annual speaker at the Dillon rally. Dillon Hall now actually builds a stage on the South Quad, and fills the evening with music, cheers, and inspiring talk. As you might expect with an undergraduate-run event, the feelings are a little more intense, and the humor a little more raw than at the university's official rally, which takes place on the Friday evening before every home game.

During the Dillon rally, you may hear more disparaging remarks about the "Alumni Dawgs" than about Notre Dame's opponent. Alumni Hall is the men's residence hall immediately adjacent to Dillon on South Quad, and it is their archrival. Every residence hall at Notre Dame has its traditional rival, and every dorm event is an occasion to insult the enemy.

FRIDAY

Noon—8:30 PM

Free shuttle to the College Football Hall of Fame. Leaves continuously from the Main Circle. On game weekends, the museum features a small exhibit on the visiting team. See Chapter Five for more details on the HOF. The trip takes 10 minutes, one-way.

3:00 PM—10:30 PM

Irish Courtyard open. This is the giant white tent in the Morris Inn's backyard. The Irish Courtyard was born because the bar inside the Morris Inn is woefully small for a football crowd. The Irish Courtyard is one of only a handful of places where you can buy mixed drinks on campus during the football weekend. The tent generally stays up for the entire football season. Live Irish music adds to the festivities from 2:30 PM to 6:30 PM. The Irish Courtyard is also open from 10:00 AM to 7:00 PM on Saturday.

4:30 PM

Open Marching Band Rehearsal. This takes place either at the band building, or on Fieldhouse Mall. The band building is at the extreme eastern edge of campus, right next to the new ROTC building. The band practices 90 minutes a day, five days a week, during football season, by the way, and all their practices are open to the public. The Friday evening practice, though, is the most popular one for football fans. This is their last practice before the pep rally.

4:45 PM—6:00 PM

Open Glee Club Rehearsal at Crowley Hall. After this rehearsal, you might want to join the Glee Club for their famous Friday Night concert during dinner in the South Dining Hall.

5:00 PM

Visiting Marching Band concert at College Football Hall of Fame. Not every visiting team brings its marching band. If they do, though, this is a great way to see them, up close and personal. They play on the Astroturf "field" that the stadium-shaped building partially encloses.

It is interesting to note the different marching band philosophies that different schools have. Big Ten schools, like Michigan and Purdue, generally have large, military-style marching bands. Smaller, more elite schools, like Stanford, tend to have rowdier, quirkier bands. The Stanford band, for example, once sparked controversy by mocking the Irish Potato Famine during a halftime show at Notre Dame. Notre Dame's band has traditionally tried to man the middle ground between these two extremes. The band members spit and polish like a Marine platoon, for example, but will also occasionally drop their horns on the field and dance.

6:20 PM

Marching Band Step Off at the Band Building. The band marches from the band building to the site of the Pep Rally.

6:30—7:00 PM

Pep Rally—Arguably the biggest event in the pre-game agenda. The location of the pep rally has been the source of some confusion in recent times. For years, Stepan Center, the geodesic dome on the northern frontier of the campus, was home to the rally. The complete lack of seating and the shockingly bad acoustics in that building forced a change. One of Bob Davies's first innovations as head coach, besides losing to Michigan State, was to move the rally to the stadium. Since then, the rallies have more or less rotated between there and the Joyce ACC. Pep Rallies are free, but those in the 12,000 seat JACC have been known to "sell out." Get there early to secure a seat.

The rallies themselves are as formatted as a Noh play. Actors include the team, cheerleaders, the band, and the leprechaun. Speakers always include the head coach, some current players, and a past player. Sometimes a surprise guest will appear, as well.

In the heat of the moment, pep rally speakers sometimes speak from their hearts instead of using their heads. The normally circumspect Lou Holtz, for example, in 1988, promised at a pep rally that Notre Dame would "beat the dog" out of the Miami Hurricanes, Notre Dame's number-one-ranked opponent. Fortunately, we did end up winning, 31-30. During the pep rally before the 1999 game against Kansas, Matt Doherty, then-Notre Dame's men's basketball coach, said that we had to beat Kansas to avenge the death of Knute Rockne, whose plane crashed in Kansas in 1931.

8:00 PM—2:00 AM

Alumni-Senior Bar open. Party with real-life students in the shadow of the stadium. Tell them what is was like "back in the day." Only students and alumni are eligible to enter, although they can sign in guests. The bar has the same schedule on Saturday.

Alumni-Senior Bar

Photo credit: Susie & Todd Tucker

SATURDAY

8:00 AM – Kickoff

Tailgating. At 6:00 AM on game day, Notre Dame Security tows every car parked in a football parking lot. At 8:00 AM, those lots open for business. For many fans, that business is tailgating. In the case of Joe Cahn, tailgating is serious business.

Joe Cahn is America's only professional tailgater. He travels the country in a custom 40-foot luxury motorcoach, evaluating tailgating at college stadiums across the country. He has appeared on *Good*

Morning America, The Today Show, ESPN, Fox Sports, and local shows all across the football-loving country. He is most famous for his annual list of the top 10 tailgating schools in the country. Joe likes to say that tailgating is the "last great American neighborhood," because of the freedom, friendliness, and hospitality that still reign in pre-game parking lots. Despite Notre Dame's Jihad on recreational vehicles—like Joe's home—he has always placed Notre Dame amongst his top five.

One of the main points of this chapter, and this book, is that there is much more to a Notre Dame football weekend than tailgating. While this is true, tailgating is an important part of the college football tradition. And, according to Joe Cahn and others, Notre Dame's is among the best. Tailgating at Notre Dame occurs wherever there are parked cars, and the prized parking lots near the stadium generally have the best tailgating. The large public lot on Juniper also has some great tailgating, although your are not within sight of the stadium. If you are lucky enough to get a space in the public lot south of the stadium, on Angela, you have the added benefit of being within walking distance of the Belmont Beverage liquor store.

There is a strong competitive element in Notre Dame tailgating. Fans try to outdo each other in all respects: who's got the biggest generator, the biggest grill, and the biggest Irish flag. With the banishment of recreational vehicles, competitive tailgaters have had to become even more creative in their drive for excess. University regulations also limit the excess. Banned items include kegs, charcoal grills, and open fires of any kind.

The typical Notre Dame tailgate party is not a drunken brawl. In fact, it is an extension of the overall family friendly mood that predominates on campus. Visiting fans usually express pleasant surprise at how nicely they are treated by Notre Dame fans.

Joe Cahn says, "tailgating is the reception. The game is the banquet." While Joe is admittedly a man who has given entirely too much thought to tailgating, he makes a great point here. While tailgating, you are free to converse, to listen, and to move around. At the banquet—the game—you are restricted by your location, and by the greater solemnity of the events. While I don't think this means you should skip the game altogether—as Joe does—I do think that you should take the time to enjoy a beer and a brat in the great northern Indiana fresh air. It is an important part of the Notre Dame weekend.

7:00 AM—7:00 PM

Cyclorama, in the north dome of the JACC. The "cyclorama" is an eight-foot high circular photograph that you stand inside. The photograph was taken on the Irish 35-yard line shortly before the kickoff of the 1994 Stanford football game. You get a full 360-degree view of a Notre Dame game from field-level. The outside of the exhibit is faced with fake brick to make it look like a stadium. While this all sounds kind of cheesy, it is actually a riveting piece of art, and if you dare to enter the cyclorama, it will change you.

The opening of the cyclorama at 7:00 AM is the first in a long series of events that takes place in the north dome—the hockey dome—of the JACC on game day. In addition to the concerts and alumni events that we will get to, the JACC is host to two "varsity shops" and a "champion tent" for Notre Dame merchandise, a full bar, a snack shop, and the Sports Heritage Hall that we covered in the last chapter.

8:00 AM—noon

Loftus Sports Center, Notre Dame's world-class indoor practice facility, open for public viewing. The facility encloses a full-size Astroturf football field, used by the football team to practice on an artificial surface for upcoming games. The building also contains the 8,000-square foot weight room used by the football team—the Haggar Fitness Center.

8:00 AM—kickoff
Eck Visitors' Center open

9:00 AM (and 10:00 AM)
St. Mary's College tour. Meet in room 122 of LeMans Hall to take
a guided tour of Notre Dame's all-woman sister school. St. Mary's, by
the way, was to become a part of Notre Dame, during Father Hesburgh's
drive to make the university co-educational. In the end, though, the
merger negotiations fell apart between the two institutions. Notre Dame
admitted women on its own in 1972, and St. Mary's has remained
all-women.

9:00 AM—1:00 PM
Alumni Hospitality Center, North Dome JACC. One of the nicest
things that happens on a football weekend is running into old friends.
Notre Dame takes extraordinary steps every game weekend to make
these reunions occur more frequently. There is a large table in the north
dome with sign-up sheets organized by class year, where alumni are
encouraged to sign in. While signing in, you can see who else from
your class is on campus for the game. In addition, the tables in the

JACC are arranged and marked by class year. Alumni can sit at their class' table, and see who else comes by.

All of these activities take place for every game. Notre Dame, in fact, never designates a "homecoming" game, because every game, really, is meant to be a homecoming for thousands of alumni.

11:00 AM
Pompon squad, formerly known as the "Dancing Irish" perform at the Notre Dame bookstore.

11:05 AM
Cheerleaders, the archrivals of the pompon squad, perform at the bookstore. This swat team of pep will freak you out with their constant unnatural smiles and their young, toned bodies.

11:55 AM
The cheerleaders and the pompon squad do it all over again, this time in the north dome of the JACC.

Noon
Shenanigans performs at the JACC. This is Notre Dame's swing choir. They sing, they dance, they display unnerving affection for show tunes.

12:30 PM
Notre Dame Glee Club concert. One of the great moments of a football weekend is hearing the Glee Club sing the Alma Mater, followed by the Victory March. You will know then that when the Shea brothers wrote the fight song in 1908, they meant it to be sung by these young men. The Glee Club will sing a number of other crowd pleasers, usually drawing a few tears with "Danny Boy."

1:00 PM
Marching Band concert on the steps of Bond Hall—the Architecture Building. For eons, this pre-game concert was held on the steps of the Main Building. During the recent renovation of that building, though,

the band moved to the steps of Bond Hall. During that two-year hiatus, the band grew, to about 300 members, and the steps of the Main Building actually shrunk. Consequently, when the building reopened in 1999, Luther Snavely, former director of Notre Dame's band, decided to keep the concert at Bond Hall.

In addition to more room for band members, the new location has more room for spectators—the grounds directly in front of the Main Building are heavily landscaped. While a concert on the steps of Bond Hall doesn't have the inherent drama of a concert on the very steps of the Golden Dome, the decision to remain in these roomier environs

was wise—the concert on the steps is one of the most popular pre-game activities. Get there early to get a good spot.

At the pre-game concert, the band will go through its usual list of Notre Dame favorites—the Victory March, "Hike Notre Dame," the Alma Mater, and "Damsha Bua" the song the band plays after every Irish victory. The band also plays the visiting team's fight song. In addition, the band will play all the music from its halftime show, complete with commentary from John Thompson, the band's own PA announcer.

After the concert on the steps, the show's not over. Some individual sections put on a show of their own in the short interval between the end of the concert and the step off to the stadium. Most notably, the Sousaphone section performs a tribute to their instrument, complete with a song of praise to Sousa's invention, performed while the section leader holds one of the sacred horns aloft. After this strange worship session, the Sousaphone players sing a clever rendition of the Fight Song—backwards. The percussion section also always puts on a sectional show, performing intricate cadences, and generally failing to prove that they can behave even more strangely than the Sousaphone section.

139

Those tall young men in kilts, by the way, are the Irish Guard. Their official role is to run interference for the Marching Band—you will see as the band fights its way through game day crowds that this is more than a formality. The other official role of the guard is to raise the American flag during the National Anthem.

Forty-five minutes before kickoff, the drum major whistles, the band members regroup, and section leaders inspect their troops. When the inspection is complete, the band marches off to the stadium, led by the Irish Guard. We should go, too—it's almost game time.

Photo courtesy of the University of Notre Dame Photography Department

Numbers you should know: 27 seconds

Daniel "Rudy" Ruettiger

Daniel "Rudy" Ruettiger became a legend among Notre Dame fans on November 8, 1975, when he played the final 27 seconds against Georgia Tech. After this, the only playing time he would receive in his career, he was carried off the field on the shoulders of his teammates, the only Notre Dame player to ever receive such a tribute. Rudy became a national legend in 1993, when the movie *Rudy* was released by Tristar Pictures.

When Reuttiger came to ND, he was 26 years old, having attended Rockport College, serving two years in the Navy, and then Holy Cross Junior College in South Bend prior to enrolling at du Lac. Although Rudy was consigned to the practice squad, Coach Dan Devine, prompted by the crowd, played Rudy for those 27 seconds—his doggedness and determination finally paying off. (Those 27 seconds were filmed for the movie in the stadium during the Boston College game.)

Today Rudy is a motivational speaker and is often sighted at games.

Rudy poses with some Notre Dame students on campus hours before the premier of the movie in downtown South Bend. Photo credit: Hans Scott Photography

Chapter Nine

FOUR QUARTERS OF TRADITION:
Inside the Stadium

NINETY MINUTES BEFORE kickoff, the gates of Notre Dame Stadium open. Notre Dame Stadium is the official name, by the way, not Knute Rockne Stadium, as is often said. The confusion arises because the stadium is so associated with Rockne and his era. He handpicked the builder, designed the stadium, and even drew up the traffic and parking scheme that remained in effect until the 1997 stadium renovation.

The traffic scheme was just one of many things changed during that two-year renovation. Even Notre Dame veterans may be thrown off by some of the massive improvements to the structure. The most immediately noticeable change is that you have to enter the stadium to even see the walls that Rockne built. The expansion totally encloses the old brick heart of the stadium.

Here is a summary of changes in the renovated stadium:

• The stadium increased its capacity from a familiar 59,075 to 80,012. Incidentally, during the renovation, the new figure was frequently said to be 80,225. This figure was based on computerized projections, and was modified after actual people began to sit in actual seats.

• All field seating and the first three rows of seats were eliminated to provide better sight lines.

• Two new scoreboards were added.

• A giant, three-tier press box with seating for 330 people was constructed on the western side of the stadium.

• Locker rooms for both Notre Dame and the visitors more than doubled in size. Tradition was carefully maintained, though—Notre Dame players still walk under the "Play Like a Champion Today" sign on their way to the field.

• Lights were installed. Previously, when Notre Dame played a night game, giant light trucks provided the illumination. These were the famous Musco Lights of Oskaloosa, Iowa. By the way, the university hardly ever schedules a true night game. The lights are necessary for afternoon games late in the season, because it gets dark so early then in South Bend.

• Eleven new openings were cut into the exterior wall of the old stadium.

• The stadium was made completely compliant with the Americans with Disabilities Act.

• The number of women's toilets was increased by over 250%.

143

NOTRE DAME STADIUM HISTORY

The vast majority of Rockne's heroics took place not at Notre Dame Stadium, but on Cartier Field. This field, located just north of the present stadium location, could accommodate only 30,000 fans. As Rockne's legend, and the legend of Notre Dame, grew, the need for a larger stadium became obvious. Rockne began to study the stadiums of his opponents as he traveled. One stadium that Rockne particularly liked was the massive stadium at the University of Michigan. Rockne sketched out a scaled-down version of Michigan's stadium, and contacted the firm that designed it—The Osborn Engineering Company, of Cleveland, Ohio. The same firm had constructed some of the other great sports edifices of the day, including Yankee Stadium, Comiskey Park, and the Polo Grounds, original home of the New York Giants.

Construction began in April 1930, and the stadium opened its gates only four months later. Rockne had the Kentucky bluegrass sod that had served him so well at Cartier carefully transferred to the new stadium.

The first game took place on October 4, 1930, when Notre Dame beat Southern Methodist University, 20-14. The official dedication game took place a week later, when Notre Dame beat Navy, 26-2. Joseph Cassanta, Class of 1923, wrote a new song in honor of the stadium's dedication—the Alma Mater. It has been performed at every game since.

That debut season would be the only season Rockne would coach in his new stadium. His plane crashed on March 31, 1931, in Bazaar, Kansas.

The stadium's first sellout came a year later, against USC. Since then, the stadium has seen more sellouts than not, and since a 1973 Thanksgiving Day matchup against Air Force, every game has been a sellout. By the time Notre Dame won its 11th National Championship in 1988, the house that Rockne built was starting to show its age.

While the issue of expanding the stadium had been bandied about for years, a 1991 resolution by the Notre Dame Alumni Association Board of Directors finally pushed the issue to the forefront. With its old capacity of 59,075, Notre Dame Stadium's capacity ranked 44th among the 107 Division I-A teams. Alumni had for years been at the mercy of a lottery to get tickets, but demand kept increasing while the stadium stayed small. In each of the five years before expansion, more money was returned to alumni with unfilled ticket orders than was kept by the university in sales. Construction on the stadium expansion began on November 6, 1995, and was completed on August 1, 1997. The stadium's re-dedication took place on September 6, 1997, with a 17-14 victory against Georgia Tech.

Photo credit: Sue & Todd Tucker

GETTING INSIDE THE STADIUM

Your ticket will have three numbers on it, in this order—a section number, a row number, and a seat number. Your ticket will not tell you what entrance to use—you will need to refer to a stadium map to figure out what entrance will be the best for you. There are five entrances to the stadium: A, B, C, D, and E. These entrances lead in to the plenum between the old stadium and the new. If your section number is three digits long, then you are in the upper section. Everyone else is in the lower section. If you are on the lower concourse—the older part of the stadium—you should find your gate, which will correspond with the section number on your ticket. If you are in the upper deck—the newer part of the stadium—then you must climb the ramps, or take the elevator to the upper part of the stadium. The only public elevator is located near sections 10 and 110 on the east side of the stadium—the side opposite the press box.

One interesting side effect of the stadium expansion is that the newer seats in the upper section are more comfortable than the older seats, which are closer to the field. This is mainly because the benches in the upper section allot several inches more to each spectator. When Rockne designed his stadium, apparently, the American rear-end was much narrower than in it is today—maybe as a result of the Great Depression. Consequently, many fans-in-the-know actually prefer the roomier, although further away, seats in the new section.

When you get to your seats, note the sections in the northwestern corner of the stadium—in the lower section only. This is the famous student section, home to the most vocal fans in the stadium. The sections are assigned by year, with seniors getting the section closest to the 50-yard line. The students, you will notice, stand for the entire game.

STADIUM RULES

Rules within the stadium are enforced by the yellow-jacketed ushers who roam the aisles. Any problems or questions can be directed to them. Here is some other important information regarding safety and stadium rules:

- Retain your ticket stub if you leave your seat.
- Doctors or others expecting calls can leave your name and seat number at the ushers' office under section 4. Or you can get a cell phone.
- No alcohol of any kind is allowed within the stadium. In fact, no glasses, bottles, or cans are permitted in the stadium.
- Smoking is not permitted in any seating area, or in the inner concourse. Smoking is allowed in the outer and upper concourses.
- No passes out will be issued.
- Throwing objects on the field is prohibited.
- Unauthorized people are not permitted on the field.
- Stadium chairs or seat backs are not permitted—cushions are okay.

SAFETY AND SECURITY

FIRST AID—There are three first aid stations within the stadium:
1. Under Section 4 in the lower concourse
2. Under Section 25 in the lower concourse
3. Outside Section 128 on the upper concourse
The first-aid stations are manned continuously by doctors, nurses, and paramedics from an hour before kick-off until the game ends.

LOST AND FOUND—The Lost and Found department is located at the Public Safety and Information Office beneath Section 27 in the lower concourse.

EATING IN THE STADIUM

One of the real weak points of the pre-renovation stadium was food service. While the quality was always good, the variety was weak— Notre Dame was the last stadium in the free world to serve Nachos—

and the concession stands were far too few. Back then, you almost had to devote an entire quarter of the game to getting your hot dog.

The renovation has helped speed up food service considerably, both by increasing the number of concession stands, and by modernizing the food preparation facilities. Concession stands can be found all around the upper and lower concourses. Fans will note that the stands are often manned by local charitable groups and churches. The university invites nonprofit groups to run stands as a fundraiser. Despite the variety of groups behind the counter, though, the menu at each stand is the same.

In addition to the concession stands, there are several well-known brand names that have their own stands around the stadium, but these tend to change from game to game. Subway has been represented at Notre Dame Stadium, and so has Ben and Jerry's. By Gate 11, on the lower concourse, Nelson's Golden Glow, a local chicken legend, maintains its very own concession stand. There you will find the one truly great bargain of Notre Dame concessions—half a chicken for $4.00.

The lines are long at all of the stands right up until halftime, when they get really long. The best times to buy food at the stadium are before kickoff, before the marching band's pre-game show, or after halftime. In the third quarter, the lines drop off to almost nothing at most stands.

Photo credit: Susie & Todd Tucker

PRE-GAME IN THE STADIUM

One of the first sights you will get of the players is during their pre-game stretching and calisthenics in the stadium—this usually takes place about an hour before kickoff. You will also get to see the visiting team doing the same thing. After that, the visiting marching band may perform a pre-game number.

Notre Dame's marching band will take the field approximately 30 minutes before the scheduled kickoff—don't miss it. While the band performs a new halftime show at every game, the pre-game show is always the same. Seeing it is like getting out the Christmas decorations—comforting and exciting at the same time.

The band assembles in the tunnel as the football teams leave the field. The first noise you will hear from them in the stadium is a cadence from the percussion section, as the band high-steps into the endzone. The band then plays its Fanfare, which is really the Fight Song, played one stanza at a time. As drum clicks keep the rhythm between stanzas, Jon Thompson introduces the band on the public address system.

After the introduction and the fanfare are complete, the band then plays "Hike, Notre Dame!" which takes the band to midfield. During this number, the band performs its notoriously difficult Hike Step: step step, shuffle shuffle. Every summer, during the band's grueling tryouts, talented musicians are turned away because they cannot master the hike step.

From midfield, the band will play the opposing team's fight song. The band, incidentally, knows a set of obscene lyrics for the fight song of almost every traditional Notre Dame foe. The band will then form into an "ND" and play the "Greatest of All College Fight Songs," the "Notre Dame Victory March."

After the Victory March, the band starts a stirringly patriotic portion of its show. While the band plays "America the Beautiful," Jon Thompson reads the Preamble to the Constitution. After this, the visiting band's conductor is usually invited to conduct the National Anthem. As the band plays The Greatest of all National Anthems, the Irish Guard hoists the flag up the stadium's main flagpole, located in the northeast corner.

My freshman year at Notre Dame was 1986, which also happened to be Lou Holtz's first year as head coach. Needless to say, there had been considerable excitement leading up to that game, which happened to be against traditional foe Michigan, then coached by the hated and feared Bo Schembechler. During this part of the pre-game show, as the band reached the final crescendo of the National Anthem, three Air Force A-10 jets flew over the stadium in formation. It seemed so perfect to me at the time, that I assumed I would see a formation of jets at every home game. I have been waiting ever since for the jets to return.

After the National Anthem, the band high steps quickly off the field, and into their seats in the stadium's northeast corner—by the flag pole. They need to hurry, because they want to be in place to play the Fight Song as the team takes the field. The visiting team will take the field first, running through the tunnel. Notre Dame fans will not boo them, and they will be cheered by the small contingent of their fans who

made the trip. After that, our men take the field, in blue jerseys, gold pants, and gold helmets.

GAME-TIME TRADITIONS

During the game, almost every action on the field is answered by a ritual in the stands. After every Irish touchdown, the band plays "Damsha Bua," better known as the "Victory Clog." The Irish Guard clog. After a field goal, or the extra point, the band plays the Fight Song. After every Irish score, the Leprechaun does push-ups equal to the total Irish score.

The band will play a number of songs during the game to keep the crowd involved, and the team inspired. One notable new addition to their repertoire is the "Imperial Death March" from *Star Wars*. The crowd, too, participates in the action, especially in the student section. You might see them at some point shaking keys in the air—this signifies a "key play" such as a third-and-long, or a going-for-it-on-fourth-down kind of situation. In the student section, students are ridiculed who ring their keys at insufficiently "key" moments.

The student section acts every game with an almost choreographed unity. During the first home game of the year, they even dress identically. This is the game of "The Shirt," a newer tradition at Notre Dame that has really taken root. Since the 1990 season, the Student Activities Board has sold a T-shirt that helps fund scholarships, service projects, and activities. In those seven years, The Shirt has raised over $1 million. The shirt is traditionally worn at the first home game. For the first several years of The Shirt, it featured a line from the Fight Song. With almost all of the Fight Song now used up, 1999's shirt featured "Love Thee Notre Dame," from the Alma Mater. The Shirt can be purchased at all the usual locations across campus, or by phone at 800-647-4641.

Half time is 20 minutes long. During this interval, the visiting marching band will play, followed by the Notre Dame band. Very often, halftime will also feature some kind of ceremony. For example, during a recent home game, the founder of The Shirt institution was given the

Harry G. Foster award. At one game a year, the marching band alumni are recognized, and they actually take the field with the band and play a number. Halftime is also notable, too, for the crush at the concession stands and in the restrooms. You are much better off watching the half-time festivities on the field, and then getting your hot dog early in the third quarter.

That voice booming across the stadium, by the way, belongs to Mike Collins. Mike is an anchorman for WSBT in South Bend, and he is also a 1967 Notre Dame graduate. Mike has been the voice of Notre Dame Stadium since 1982, when he took over the job from the legendary Frank Crosair. Frank announced every single home game from 1948 to 1981.

Photo credit: Vince Wehby, Jr.

Between the third and fourth quarter, the band plays the rousing "1812 Overture." The entire student section will make the "tomahawk" chopping motion with their arms in time with the music. For many years, they held the fingers of their chopping hand in an "L" shape, signifying "Lou," for Coach Lou Holtz. Some students now hold their fingers in a "b" shape, for Bob Davies, but it hasn't really caught on.

During the fourth quarter, an Indiana State Trooper, Officer Tim McCarthy, will be introduced on the public address system, to rousing applause. His job is to give a safe driving message late in the game, usually re-inforced with an extremely corny joke. Example: "Weaving in and out of traffic will make you a basket case." The crowd loves him.

After the game is over, a few traditions remain to be acted out. Notre Dame fans rarely tear down the goalposts, although it has been known to happen. Before the team leaves the field, they will gather in the northwest corner, in front of the student section, and raise their helmets, to salute their fans. The band then takes the field to one of the lesser-known Irish football songs, "When Irish Backs Go Marching By." They'll play the "1812 Overture" again, then the Alma Mater, and then the Fight Song. Only after victories, the band will then play "Damsha Bua," and the Irish Guard will clog away, right on the 50-yard line. The band leaves the field playing "On Down the Line."

Game day is over, so it's time for us to get on down the line. Drive safe, and come back soon.

154

Numbers you should know: 2

New Traditions

Notre Dame's rich game day traditions have only gotten richer with change in two of its hallowed institutions—the Leprechaun and the Irish Guard.

Michael Brown—Class of 2001

In 1999, the first African-American to portray the Leprechaun mascot was selected. Michael Brown, from Milwaukee, Wisconsin, represents the 22nd student to wear the lucky costume of lore. Selected as a junior to portray the spirited little fella, Brown held onto his role as a senior too, thanks to his amazing athleticism, energy, charm, and ability to work up a crowd. Although there

Photo credit: Peter Richardson

have been previous mascots without red-hair and freckles and names that begin with "Mc" or "O'" since the Leprechaun jumped on the Irish scene in the mid-'60s, Brown's selection was a big bound forward in recognizing the value of (and need for) diversity at the university.

Molly Kinder—Class of 2001

Though they have always worn skirts, the members of the famed Irish Guard have been all-male since formation of the statutesque troup in 1951…all-male, that is, until 6-3, senior Molly Kinder changed all that in 2000 and high-stepped into Notre Dame history as the first female member of the Irish Guard. Although women were first enrolled at ND in 1974, no Irish lasses appeared on the squad largely due to the lofty height requirements. Molly, a government and international relations major from Williamsville, New York, practiced for fall tryouts marching through in the streets of Chile where she studied abroad in the summer of 2000 and she donned the official uniform for

Photo credit: Peter Richardson

the first time at the first home football game against Texas A& M on September 2.

An editorial in the September 1 edition of *The Observer* stated: "Although a female member of the Guard changes its all-male history, it does not have to change the tradition of Irish Guard as honorable representatives of the University...the Irish Guard promotes pride and respect; both of these qualities transcend gender lines."

And Molly Kinder certainly stands tall as an exemplary representative of Notre Dame and of the Irish Guard, as she makes her mark in history with determination, talent, and class and proves once again that change can be beautiful.

Chapter Ten

AFTER THE GAME

AS WE DRIVE AWAY from the emptying stadium, we should look back, and discuss the game in detail: the blown calls, the great tackles, the marching band's performance, the bowl implications. It might be a good idea to perform the same kind of review on this book.

A goal I had in mind when I started this project was to describe the perfect Notre Dame weekend. I found out soon, though, that the perfect weekend is very much in the eye of the beholder. Some fans want to stay cheap at the Motel 6—others will want to be surrounded by ND celebrities and luxury at the pricey Varsity Clubs of America. Some fans will want to eat a $30 steak at Tippecanoe's—others will want to eat a bowl of Cap'n Crunch in the South Dining Hall. It's not just economic tastes that vary, either. Being part of a sweaty, shouting mob at Corby's will be the highlight of the weekend to some, an unspeakable horror to others. I hope that my book will help each of you construct a perfect weekend, even though each of you will have to decide for yourself exactly what that is. A perfect weekend, then, is a personal matter.

A perfect season, though, is a matter of record, and I can write with some authority about that—I was there for the last one. That championship 1988 season was the football highlight of my four years at ND, the football Big Bang that in some way led, 12 years later, to the writing of this book.

They were good years to be a student at the University of Notre Dame. My first year was also Lou Holtz's first year as head coach—1986. We were five and six that year, the same record as Faust's final year, but I didn't know a single person who didn't believe that Coach Holtz was going to bring us back. It didn't take him very long.

During my sophomore year, we had a better record, and a Cotton Bowl bid. The real landmark, though, was Tim Brown winning the Heisman Trophy. During the ceremony, a representative from the Downtown Athletic Club said that any time Notre Dame wins something, it's good for college football—a phrase I repeat often to my non-Notre Dame friends. Tim Brown lived in my hall—Cavanaugh Hall. He graciously signed the *Sports Illustrated* cover that hangs above my desk to this day.

Nineteen-eighty-eight was my junior year. We won a record eight games at home that year, capped by the Miami game, which we won 31-30. Although Notre Dame was never behind in that game, it was a nail biter until the last play. I called my father after the game, but he hadn't seen the ending—he said that he had to turn the television off because the game was too stressful to watch.

Shortly after Christmas that year, I took a Greyhound bus from Louisville, Kentucky, to Kansas City. From there, Sean O'Connell and I drove to Tempe, Arizona, in his sister's Tercel. On the first frosty night of the drive, we pulled into a rest stop in Kansas. It was, we discovered, the Knute Rockne Memorial Rest Stop. When we asked the attendant why, he pointed into the blackness that he said contained a cornfield—that's where the Rock's plane crashed. He spoke in such a way that I believed, had it been daylight, I might have seen tendrils of smoke still climbing from the wreckage.

Sean O'Connell, still the funniest person I have ever known, made the drive go fast. In Tempe, our friends gradually straggled in from across the country, to watch that final game in the desert. In Sun Devil Stadium, we watched the Irish defeat West Virginia, the last game of a perfect season, a National Championship season.

During that year, I worked in the Oak Room during the week. The

Oak Room was almost never crowded, so I had plenty of time to discuss the season with the students and faculty that wandered in from the cold. As the season marched on, and we remained undefeated, a priest once told me over coffee that the numbers were in our favor: we had won championships in 1966 and 1977. Nineteen-eighty-eight would be a natural continuation of that series. I thought about that last championship, the 1977 championship under head coach Dan Devine. Certainly we were due—11 years had passed. A lifetime, an eternity.

That was 13 years ago.

As a student, the fundamentals of going to a game are much easier—you never have to give a thought to getting tickets, driving to the stadium, or finding a parking space. Going to the game as a full-blown adult is difficult on another, more problematic level, as well. When I first came back to the stadium, a year after graduation, the people I sat near seemed shockingly sedate compared to the fans I had cheered with for four years in the student section. I remember being disappointed when they all sat down after the National Athem. Eventually, I sat down, too, after what I thought was a suitable delay. I was surrounded by boring old people, and I was terrified that I might be mistaken for one.

In 10 short years, though, I have become fairly comfortable with being boring and old. I have even discovered some advantages to being a 32 year old at the games. I generally have more beer money these days. I don't have to worry about all the tests I should be studying for, or the papers I should be writing. The ushers are nicer to me. All in all, though, I'd rather be 20 years old.

I hope this book makes all of those other things easier for everybody—the parking, the tickets, getting a room, getting home. I hope everybody that reads this can step away from the stresses of their daily lives for a weekend to drive north, to have a perfect football weekend, whether they come by private jet or interurban electric train. Or Toyota Tercel.

So what is my perfect game day? That's easy. I am in the stands with Trent, Steve, Greg, Sean, the Yeti, and the rest. Patty, Kathy, and their gang are there too, rolling their eyes at our jokes, already making plans for after the game. Sean, thank God, has smuggled in some whiskey, because we're about halfway through the season, and the afternoons are starting to cool off. We are undefeated so far, and championship talk and bowl scenarios buzz through the crowd. Notre Dame wins the toss, we take the kick, and we all cheer, happy to be alive and together. At the perfect game, I am always surrounded by my friends. There is a chill in the air, and a National Championship dead ahead.

CAMPUS MAP

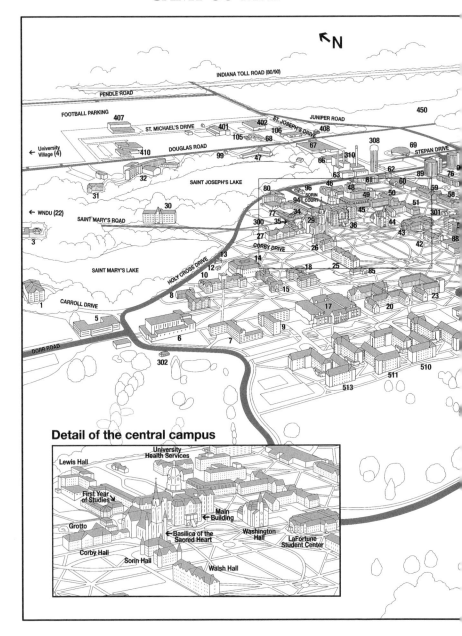

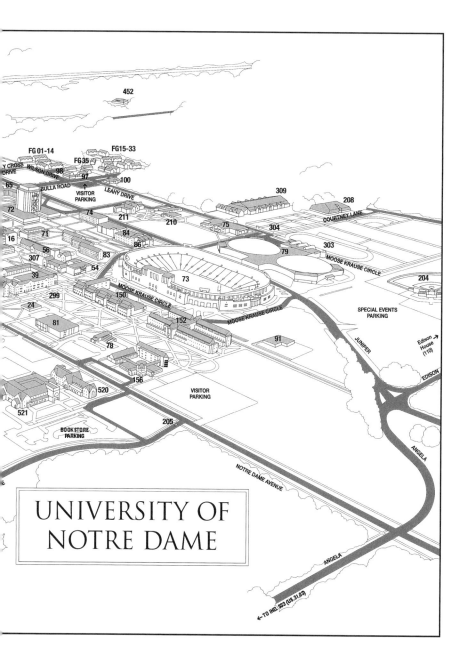

UNIVERSITY OF
NOTRE DAME

CAMPUS MAP LEGEND

1 Carroll Hall	43 LaFortune Student Center
3 Fatima Retreat House and Shrine	44 Washington Hall
4 University Village	45 St. Edward's Hall
5 Campus Security Building	46 University Health Services
6 Rockne Memorial	47 Holy Cross House
7 Pangborn Hall	48 Stanford Hall
8 Lyons Hall	49 Keenan Hall
9 Fisher Hall	50 Zahm Hall
10 Morrissey Hall	51 Cavanaugh Hall
12 Log Chapel	52 Nieuwland Science Hall
13 Old College	53 Riley Hall of Art and Design
14 Bond Hall (Architecture)	54 Snite Museum of Art
15 Howard Hall	56 O'Shaughnessy Hall
16 Stepan Chemistry Hall	58 Breen-Phillips Hall
17 South Dining Hall	59 Farley Hall
18 Badin Hall	60 North Dining Hall
19 Coleman-Morse Center (Spring 2001)	61 Haggar Hall
20 Dillon Hall	62 Fire Station
21 Morris Inn	63 Power Plant
22 WNDU Radio and Television	64 Pasquerilla Hall East
23 Alumni Hall	65 Knott Hall
24 Post Office	66 Hessert Aerospace Research Center
25 Walsh Hall	67 Facilities/Maintenance Center
26 Sorin Hall	68 Reyniers Life Building
27 Corby Hall	69 Stepan Center
29 Basilica of the Sacred Heart	70 Center for Social Concerns
30 Columba Hall	71 Radiation Research Building
31 Sacred Heart Parish Center	72 Hesburgh Library
(St. Joseph Hall)	73 Stadium
32 Moreau Seminary	74 Computing Center and Mathematics
34 First Year of Studies	Building
35 Presbytery	75 Rolfs Sports Recreation Center
36 Main Building	76 Pasquerilla Hall West
37 Law School	77 Earth Sciences Building
39 Fitzpatrick Hall of Engineering	78 University Club
40 Cushing Hall of Engineering	79 Joyce Center (Joyce Athletic and
41 Hurley Hall	Convocation Center)
42 Crowley Hall of Music	80 Lewis Hall

81 McKenna Hall (Center for Continuing Education)
83 Decio Faculty Hall
84 Freimann Life Science Center/ Galvin Life Science Center
85 Knights of Columbus Council Hall
86 Hank Family Center for Environmental Sciences
88 Hayes-Healy Center
89 Flanner Hall
90 Grace Hall
91 Alumni-Senior Club
94 Brownson Hall
96 Laundry Pick-up Center
96 Mail Distribution Center
97 O'Hara-Grace Graduate Residences
98 Wilson Commons
99 Province Archives Center
100 Early Childhood Development Center
105 Reyniers Life Annex
106 Notre Dame Credit Union
110 Edison House
150 DeBartolo Hall
152 College of Business
156 Hesburgh Center for International Studies
204 Eck Baseball Stadium
205 Main Gate
206 East Gate
208 Eck Tennis Pavilion
209 Siegfried Hall
210 Band Building
211 Pasquerilla Center (ROTC)
299 Sesquicentennial Common
300 Grotto of Our Lady of Lourdes
301 Clarke Memorial Fountain/ Fieldhouse Mall
302 Burke Memorial Golf Course
303 Cartier Field/Krause Stadium
304 Courtney Tennis Center

307 Shaheen Mestrovic Memorial
308 Water Tower
309 Haggar Fitness Complex/ Loftus Sports Center/ Meyo Field
310 Facilities Building
401 St. Michael's Laundry
402 Mason Support Services Center
407 Food Services Support Facility
408 Paris House (Midwest Hispanic Catholic Commission)
410 Ave Maria Press
450 Warren Golf Course
452 Warren Golf Club House
510 Keough Hall
511 O'Neill Hall
512 Welsh Hall
513 McGlinn Hall
520 Notre Dame Alumni Association/ Eck Notre Dame Visitors' Center
521 Hammes Notre Dame Bookstore

FG35 Fischer Graduate Community Center
FG01-FG33 Fischer Graduate Residences

STADIUM SEATING MAP

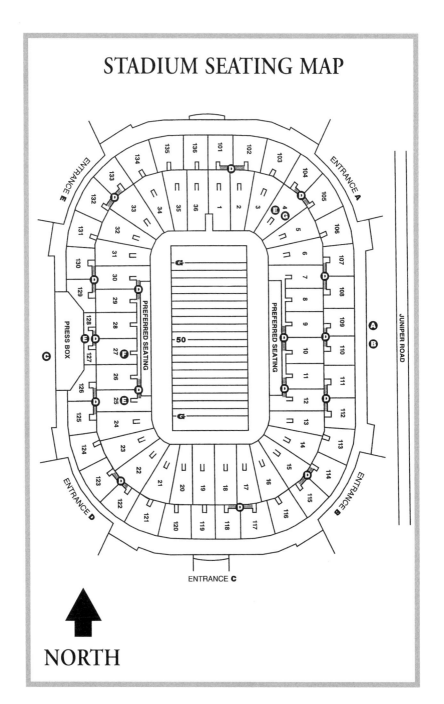

ENTRANCE E

ENTRANCE A

ENTRANCE D

ENTRANCE B

ENTRANCE C

JUNIPER ROAD

PRESS BOX

PREFERRED SEATING

NORTH

167

FUTURE FOOTBALL SCHEDULES

2001

September 8
at Nebraska

September 15
at Purdue

**September 22
Michigan State**

September 29
at Texas A&M

**October 6
Pittsburgh**

**October 13
West Virginia**

**October 20
USC**

October 27
at Boston College

**November 3
Tennessee**

**November 17
Navy**

November 24
at Stanford

2002

**September 7
Purdue**

**September 14
Michigan**

September 21
at Michigan State

**October 5
Stanford**

**October 12
Pittsburgh**

October 19
at Air Force

October 26
at Florida State

**November 2
Boston College**

November 9
at Navy (site TBA)

**November 23
Rutgers**

November 30
at USC

2003

September 13
at Michigan

**September 20
Michigan State**

September 27
at Purdue

**October 4
Wake Forest**

October 11
at Pittsburgh

**October 18
USC**

October 25
at Boston College

**November 1
Florida State**

**November 8
Navy**

**November 15
BYU**

November 22
at Syracuse

November 29
at Stanford

ABOUT THE AUTHOR

Todd Tucker graduated from Notre Dame in 1990 with a degree in history. After graduation, he entered the Navy's demanding Nuclear Propulsion program, eventually completing six patrols onboard the legendary submarine the *USS Alabama*. With the Cold War safely won, Todd returned to Indiana with his family in 1995.

Todd's travel writing has appeared in a number of national magazines, including *The Rotarian, Inside Sports, Historic Traveler*, and *TWA Ambassador*. This is his first book.

INDEX

Air Force Academy 5
Allegro Subs 86
Allie's American Grill 55
Alma Mater 146, 152
Alumni Hall 128
Alumni-Senior Club 89-90
American Eagle 18
Angela Road 104
Anthony Travel 10
Army 29, 30, 63-64
ATA Connection 18

Badin Hall 109
Baylor 9
Bazaar, Kansas 4, 146
Bed and Breakfasts 56-58
Bella, Janice 34
Belmont Beverage 133
Bendix Field 28
Bertelli, Angelo 124
Best Inn 40
Best Western 48
Best, Bob 78
Beverly Shores, Indiana 22
Blanchard, Doc 63
Blue and Gold Game 13
Boathouse 116
Bond Hall 91, 137
Book Inn 57-58
Bowden, Bobby 70
Bridget McGuire's 93
Bristol, Indiana 61
Brown, Michael 155-156
Brown, Tim 126, 159
Bruno's 96

Bryant, Bear 1, 121
BW-3 100

Café De Grasta 91
Café Poche 91
Café SBN 17
Cahn, Joe 132-133, 135
California 1
Campgrounds 60-61
Campus Map 162-165
Campus Tour 103-123
Candlelight Buffet 80, 85-86
Cap N' Cork 93
Cap'n Crunch 79
Carlton Lodge 50
Carroll Hall 115
Cartier Field 144
Cavanaugh Hall 159
Cassanta, Joseph 146
Chicago 1, 19-22
Chicago O'hare Airport 17, 18
Chicago Tribune 9
Cincinnati, Ohio 18
CJ's Pub 94
Clark Memorial Fountain 118-119
Clarke, Maude 118
Cleveland, Ohio 18
Coach's 94
College Football Hall of Fame 11, 55, 65-76, 97, 98, 129, 130
College of Business Administration 91, 123
Collins, Mike 153
Columba Hall 115
Common Stock 91

Connor, Jack 64
Continental Express 18
Corby's 92-93, 158
Corporate Wings 28
Courtyard by Marriott 48
Coveleski Regional Baseball
    Stadium 76
Cram, Ralph Adams 80
Crenshaw, Ben 116
Crosair, Frank 153
Crowley, Jim 14
Cyclorama 135

"Damshua Bua" 139, 152
Davies, Bob 131, 153
Davis, Glen 63
Daylight Savings Time 26-27
Days Inn 42-43
Days Inn, Elkhart 59
Days Inn, Plymouth 59
DeBartolo Quad 24, 122-123
DeBartolo, Ed Jr. 122
DeBartolo, Ed Sr. 122
Delta Connection 18
Detroit, Michigan 18
Devine, Dan 101, 141, 160
Dillon Hall 128
Dining 79-100
Dining Halls 80-86
Dining, Off Campus 92-100
Dining, On Campus 79-92
Doherty, Matt 131
Douglas Road 104
Driving to Notre Dame 22-23

East Race Waterway 74
Eby's Pines Campground 61
Eck Tennis Pavilion 109

Eck Visitors Center 104, 106, 136
Eck, Frank 106
Edison Road 104
Elkhart, Indiana 59-60
Emporium 100

Fairfield Inn 50
Farley Hall 84
Fatima Retreat House and
    Shrine 115
Faust, Gerry 159
Fieldhouse Mall 118-119
Fire Station 116
Flanner Hall 116
Florida State 23-24
Flying to Notre Dame 16-18
Forward Pass 3
Four Horsemen 14-15
Fraternities 31
Future ND Schedules 169

Gary, Indiana 22
Georgia Tech 70
Gipp, George 29-30
Gipper's Lounge 41
Glee Club 130, 137
Golf 116-118
Grace Hall 116
Grambling 69
Green Field 24, 123
Greenfield's Café 91
Gregori, Luis 112
Grotto 113-114

Haggar Fitness Center 135
Hammes Bookstore 106,107
Hampton Inn and Suites 43-44
Hampton Inn, Elkhart 59

Hampton Inn, Mishawaka 52
Handicapped Accessibility 13
Hart, Leon 124
Hayes, Woody 71, 73
Heavens, Jerome 30
Heisman Trophy 1, 63, 71, 104, 124-126, 159
Hesburgh Center 91, 123
Hesburgh, Father Theodore M. 119,136
Highway 31 10, 11, 22, 35, 36
Hike Notre Dame 139, 150
Hoffman, Emil T. 88
Holiday Inn Express, Elkhart 60
Holiday Inn Express, Mishawaka 49
Holiday Inn, Downtown 55-56
Holiday Inn, Plymouth 59
Holiday Inn, University Area 40-41
Holtz, Lou 101-102, 131, 151, 153, 159
Holy Cross College 24
Holy Cross Hall 15
Hornung, Paul 125
Howard Hall 109-110
Howard Johnson 38
Huarte, John 126
Huddle 86-87, 88
Huddle Mart 86-87
Hudson Lake, Indiana 22

Indiana 1
Indiana Toll Road 23,35
Indianapolis, Indiana 22
Inn at St. Mary's 34-35
Irish Café 91
Irish Guard 140, 156-157
Irish Sports Report 10

Jackson, Keith 71
Jamison Inn 33-34,47
Joyce ACC 8, 119, 120-122, 131, 135, 136
Joyce, Father Ned 121
Juniper Road 104

Kegs 134
Kentucky Bluegrass 144
Kernan, Joe 65
Kinder, Molly 156
Kish, Bernie 66,73
Knights Inn, Elkhart 59
Knights Inn, Highway 31 38-39
KOA Campground, Elkhart County 61
KOA Campground, South Bend East 60-61
Kokomo, Indiana 22
K's Grill & Pub 98-99

La Esperanza 99
Lake Effect Snow 27
Lattner, John 124
Laurium, Michigan 29
Law School 91
Layden, Elmer 14
Leahy, Frank 3, 63-64, 101, 116
Leahy's 89
Leahy's Lads 136
Linebacker 93
Livingston, John and Peggy 57
Lodging 31-62
Loftus Sports Center 135
Long Island 1
Lost and Found 148
Lottery 6

LSU 9
Luecke, Steve 67
Lujack, Johnny 63, 124
Lux, Bob 46
Lyon's Hall 109

Macri's 95
Main Building 110-112
Main Street, Mishawaka 53
Mandarin House 100
Marching Band 130, 131, 137, 150
Marriott, Downtown 54-55, 67
McCarthy, Tim 154
McGraw, Pat 34
Medhurst, Bob and Pauline 56
Michiana Regional Airport
    16-18, 28
Michigan 1, 12, 70
Michigan Avenue, Chicago 22
Michigan State 77, 126
Midway Airport 17
Miller, Don 14
Mishawaka 45-46
Monohan, Richard and Venera 58
Montana, Joe 122
Moreau Seminary 115
Morris Inn 32-33, 34, 35, 47, 62,
    88-89, 129
Morris, Ernest 33
Morrissey Hall 109
Motel 6, Highway 31 44-45, 158
Motel 6, Plymouth 59
Musuraca, Jim 34

National Championships 63, 77,
    101-102, 146, 158, 161
Naval Academy 12
NBC 2

Nebraska 14
New Orleans 1
New York 1
Nick's Patio 100
Nicola's 99
North Dining Hall 82, 84-86
Northern Indiana Center for
    History 76
Northwest/KLM 18
Notre Dame Avenue 104
Notre Dame Shift 3
Notre Dame Stadium 142-154
"Notre Dame Victory March"
    70, 139, 150
Notre Dame's Era of Ara 78

Oak Room 80, 83, 159-160
Observer, The 12, 128
Oliver Inn Bed and Breakfast 58
Osborn Engineering Company 144
O'Shaughnessy Hall 91
Outback 96

Pagna, Tom 78
Parents Day 7-8, 11
Parisi's 99
Parking 13, 24-25
Parseghian, Ara 77-78, 101
Pendle Road Lot 24
Pep Rally 131-132
Pit 91-92
Pittsburgh, Pennsylvania 18
PJ's Sports Tours 10
Plymouth, Indiana 59
Prentkowski, Dave 82, 86
Private aircraft 28
Purdue University 1

Queen Anne Inn Bed and
    Breakfast 56

Ramada Inn 41
Randall Inn 38
Randolph Street, Chicago 22
Reagan, Ronald 106
Recker, Clement 87
Recker's 83,87
Recreational Vehicles 23, 60, 127,
    133,134
Redden Travel 10
Residence Halls, staying in 61-62
Rice, Grantland 14
Robinson, Eddie 69
Rocco's 98
Rockne Memorial Gym 109
Rockne, Knute 3, 14, 17, 29, 101,
    132, 144, 159
"Rocky Top" 70
Rolf's Aquatic Center 109
Rose Bowl 14
ROTC at Notre Dame 118
ROTC Building 103
Rudy 92-93,141
Rutgers 12
R-Zone 87

Sacred Heart Basilica 112
Scalping 8, 10-12
Schembechler, Bo 151
Season Tickets 6
Seating in the stadium 147
Security Building 114-115
Sesquicentennial Common 123
Shenanigans 137
Signature Inn 37-38
Snowfall 28

Soldier Field 22
Sorin, Father 16, 110-111
Sorin's 88
South Bend Chocolate Company
    74, 97-98
South Bend Tribune 9
South Dining Hall 80-82, 87, 159
South Shore Railroad 16-22
Sports Heritage Hall 121
St. Joseph Hall 115
St. Joseph's Lake 115-116
St. Louis, Missouri 18
St. Mary's College 7, 23, 25, 136
St. Mary's Lake 114-115
Stadium Expansion 2, 8, 142-143,
    146
Stadium rules 148
Stadium Safety and Security 148
Stadium Seating Chart 167
Stanford 14
Stepan Center 116, 131
Stonehenge 118-119
Strickler, George 14
Studebaker National Museum 75
Studebagels 100
Studebaker, Clement 95-96
Studio Plus 47
Stuhldreher, Harry 14
Super 8, Elkhart 60
Super 8, Highway 31 42
Super 8, Mishawaka 52-53
Super 8, Plymouth 59

Tailgating 127, 132-135
Tarner, Mark 75
Temperature 27
Theodore M. Hesburgh Library
    119-120
Thompson, John 139, 150

Ticket Brokers 8-9
Ticket Office 8
Tickets 5-13
Tickets, Alumni 6-7
Tickets, Face Value 5
Tickets, Students 5,11
Tippecanoe Place 95-96, 158
Tokyo 55
Tomassito's 86
Touchdown Jesus 120
Traffic Patterns 25-26
Transpo City Busses 16
Travel Agents 9
TWA 18

United Express 18
United Limousine 17
University of Alabama 1
University Club 90
US Airways 18
US Steel 22
USC 3, 22

Varsity Clubs of America 46, 158
Vine 97

Waddick's 91
Wake Forest 12
Warren Golf Course 116-118
Warren Grille 117
Weather 27-28
"When Irish Backs Go Marching
     By" 154

Yankee Stadium 63, 144

JOIN US AFTER
THE GAME
FOR AN ELEGANT
CANDLELIGHT
DINNER IN
THE NORTH OR
SOUTH
DINING HALLS

A PRE-GAME BRUNCH IS OFFERED IN THE
NORTH & SOUTH DINING HALLS